In loving memory of Flar 7

ABOUT THE AUTHOR

Tammy Sullivan (Tennessee) has been practicing Witchcraft for over a decade. She has written articles for *FATE* magazine, *Circle Magazine*, and many Llewellyn annuals, including the *Witches' Spell-a-Day Almanac*, *Wicca Almanac*, and *Magical Almanac*.

TO WRITE TO THE AUTHOR

If you wish to contact the author or would like more information about this book, please write to the author in care of Llewellyn Worldwide and we will forward your request. Both the author and publisher appreciate hearing from you and learning of your enjoyment of this book and how it has helped you. Llewellyn Worldwide cannot guarantee that every letter written to the author can be answered, but all will be forwarded. Please write to:

Tammy Sullivan

^c/o Llewellyn Worldwide

2143 Wooddale Drive, Dept. 0-7387-0891-7

Woodbury, Minnesota 55125-2989, U.S.A.

Please enclose a self-addressed stamped envelope for reply, or $1.00 to cover costs. If outside U.S.A., enclose international postal reply coupon.

ELEMENTAL
WITCH

FIRE   AIR   WATER   EARTH
DISCOVER YOUR NATURAL AFFINITY

TAMMY SULLIVAN

Llewellyn Publications
Woodbury, Minnesota

First Edition
First Printing, 2006

Book design by Donna Burch
Cover design by Gavin Dayton Duffy
Cover illustration © Imagezoo
Edited by Andrea Neff
Illustration on page 18 by Llewellyn Art Department

Llewellyn is a registered trademark of Llewellyn Worldwide, Ltd.

ISBN-13: 978-0-7387-0891-1
ISBN-10: 0-7387-0891-7

Llewellyn Publications
A Division of Llewellyn Worldwide, Ltd.
2143 Wooddale Drive, Dept. 0-7387-0891-7
Woodbury, Minnesota 55125-2989, U.S.A.
www.llewellyn.com

Printed in the United States of America

OTHER BOOKS BY TAMMY SULLIVAN

Pagan Anger Magic: Positive Transformations from Negative Energies
(Citadel Press, 2005)

ACKNOWLEDGMENTS

Special thanks to Sister Earth, Sister Fire, and Sister Water.

Special thanks to my editor, Andrea Neff, for her patience, support, and talent.

CONTENTS

NOTE ABOUT HERBS

All herbal formulas in this book are given for historic understanding and reference. No herbal formula should be consumed unless specifically stated. Herbs and herbal formulas that are potentially toxic are stated, and the author and publisher assume no responsibility for those who consume such preparations in any dose. People with allergies or sensitive skin should take caution when using herbal remedies. Do not take any herb or herbal preparation without direct consultation from a qualified health care provider. In no way is this material a substitute for trained medical or psychological care. This book is intended to be used by stable, mature adults seeking personal awareness and transformation.

1

INTRODUCTION

Sea Witch, Water Witch, Fire Witch, Air Witch, Earth Witch . . . Who are all of these people? They aren't cartoon characters or players in a role-playing game. They are Witches with a magical twist. They work directly with a preferred element. Their world is a magical mix of folklore and truths, and their magic is beautiful and fantastic. Watching a Sea Witch conduct a ritual on the beach can be a moving experience. You can almost see the Witch become the mermaid. You can envision smiling dolphins jumping out of the surf, as if popping up to say hello just to her. The Sea Witch is an expert on the magic and wisdom of water. She can tell you all you want to know about wishing wells, fountains, and tidal waves. Elemental Witches bond so closely with their element that they carry the characteristics of it.

Choosing an elemental specialty is becoming a common practice in Witchcraft today. It helps seekers personalize their paths and define their goals, while giving them an edge when it comes to magical work. It gives them a specialized area of knowledge.

Practitioners are deepening and individualizing their paths in varied ways. Some are choosing to add a lunar/solar influence and classify themselves as a Dark or Light Witch, while others prefer to seek a matron/patron deity to deepen their craft. It's not unusual today to meet a fellow Witch who identifies her path by calling herself a Dark Green Witch. What this label means is she works mainly with a lunar influence and also primarily with the earth element. Some may add a bit more to that by naming their patron or matron deity.

Wicca and Witchcraft are sometimes viewed as conformist paths, especially within traditions, but they don't have to be. Solitary Eclectic Wicca is a spiritual path that encourages you to search your soul to determine your exact path, as no two paths should be exactly alike. Choosing to add an elemental affinity can be a way to further develop your unique path.

The practice of Elemental Witchcraft need not be solitary. Today, there are whole covens being formed by those with the same elemental affinity. Sometimes they include within their ranks those of a differing element, to maintain balance within the group environment.

In chapter 2, you will find tools, such as quizzes and questionnaires, to help you determine your predominant element. Personality quirks and even favorite colors can all be hidden clues to an affinity you may not have noticed before.

Meditation, vision questing, and soul-searching are among the techniques used to determine an affinity. It is possible to have more than one affinity, although rarely will the two be tied for first place. You do not have to choose just one, although you will more than likely wish to work with one at a time.

Astrology may play into your elemental preference. For example, I have a Sagittarius Sun with an Aquarius Moon. I have a distinct preference for the element of air (my Moon sign), followed by fire (my Sun sign). In my case, the two elements are reversed in order of preference compared to my birth chart. In some cases, the sign/element combinations may not fit at all, such as a Taurus (earth sign) friend of mine who has a distinct preference for fire. In other cases, they may follow the birth chart exactly, such as a friend of mine with a Libra Sun (air sign) and a Pisces Moon (water sign). She considers air to be her predominant element, followed by water.

Any elemental preference may coincide with indications in the birth chart, but more often than not, affinities come from a deeper source within the subconscious of the seeker. I have noticed that some people do eventually gravitate to their birth element (Sun sign). Often, they have things to overcome first. There may be a strength issue. A woman I know felt a definite pull toward fire, but felt she was not strong enough to work with it. Fire had always made her nervous, though excited too. She began with earth instead and from there progressed to water and air, saving fire for last. By the time she got to fire, she was ready to handle it and has an amazing kinship with fire magic today.

Since Elemental Witchcraft is so personally defined, this book is intended only as an outline for the development of your path. It is not meant to *be* your path, but only to help you further define and personalize it by giving you ideas and examples. Any other little tweaks you decide to incorporate are fine. It is your path and no one else can tell you how to walk it.

Keep in mind that it is possible to outgrow an elemental connection over time and move on to a new elemental preference entirely. Some Witches choose to work with elemental combinations, such as storms. Still others specialize in alternate elements. An Iron Witch or an Ice Witch is no longer unheard of. Your specialty should be unique to you.

For the purposes of this book, we will be discussing earth, air, fire, and water as the primary elements. While it is commonly accepted that spirit is the fifth element, spirit comes into play in any spiritual path, so it will not be treated as a separate element here.

In your studies, you may have happened upon other systems, such as feng shui, that assert the primary elements to be earth, water, wood, metal, and fire. The Celtic system of magic uses nine elements: earth, air, water, stars, sun, moon, rock, fire, and lightning. Then there is the Nordic system, which counts fire, ice, air, and water. While you may choose to add ice as a specialty of your path, I suggest you learn water and air first. Ice is the result of two combined primaries.

Elemental Witchcraft works in different ways for different people. It all depends on what you want from it. It can either define your path or subdefine it. In other words, it can be an added personalization or it can *be* the path. For instance, I am an Air Witch, yet I have a matron goddess as well. My affinity to air is an added definition of my path, not the extent of it. Your path can be either—the choice is yours.

I personally recommend using the elemental influence as a sub-definition of your path. This approach helps you maintain a balance and a clearer focus. However, accepting an elemental affinity as the main focus of your path can make way for some magic that those of us striving for balance may not achieve. Giving yourself over to an element does indeed open new doorways, although that is not always such a beneficial thing. We are human and live on Earth; therefore, we must accept our limits. Knowledge is key, and no element will allow itself to be used in a way that does not fit with its attributes. If the element decides to work with you, you must always be respectful. When embracing your personal element to such an extent, the gains could be magnificent but the price too high for a human. Set your limits, even with your preferred element.

You must also seek to maintain a balance with the other elements. An elemental imbalance in the body can deplete your energy and cause lightheadedness, improper expression of emotion, and weight gain, to name just a few possibilities. Having a predominant element does not mean the element should be exclusive. Our bodies are made of all four elements, each element ruling its own vital function within us to create one whole being. We cannot just ignore our circulatory system; likewise we cannot ignore any one element, and it would be foolhardy to try.

The four elements are all tied together in nature, and everything is tied to the fifth element, spirit. Following the element of spirit is something we all naturally do within our seeking. Having faith in any religious doctrine or set of beliefs *is* following the element of spirit. Dreaming is also following the element of spirit. Spirit comes into play in everything we do, as long as we accept it. In order for Elemental Witchcraft to work, it all begins with the fifth element. Spirit is the alpha and omega of Witchcraft. Since spirit is tied to the world at large and is all-encompassing, it is impossible to miss.

Native Americans have wondrous control when it comes to working with the elements for magical purposes. To this day they maintain the ability to call the elements together to meet their needs, by performing a rain dance, for example. Seeking to control an element is not always the smartest move, though. It is much easier to work with it. You can no more force an element to do your bidding than you can turn yourself inside out. It is a partnership, one in which you are the seeker and the element holds the highest card.

Herbs play a special role in Elemental Witchcraft. While you might think that they would automatically fall under the rule of earth, they do not. It takes all four elements for an herb to grow. Earth, air, water, and sunlight (fire) all are necessary, and all herbs contain the element of spirit. However, herbs do fall into elemental categories according to their predominant qualities and magical uses. You will find herbal correspondences listed in the four elemental magic chapters.

Color plays a significant role in an elemental specialty, as color is not ruled by any one element. Remember, it takes three elements to make a rainbow. Certain colors have specific attributes and work more harmoniously with a particular element. You will find these color affinities listed in the elemental magic chapters as well.

The same is true of stones and crystals. It takes all four elements to create a crystal. Crystals, like herbs, are not exclusive to the earth element; thus, they are used for magical purposes in all of the elemental paths, and each one has specific magical qualities. These are also listed within the elemental magic chapters.

The human senses and universal laws even play roles in elemental specialties. Learning to work magic in harmony with the predominant element in your life can be powerful and life-affirming. It is wise to approach elemental specialties as an exploration. To achieve harmony with an element, you must first know the element. Over time, your perception of the element will change. This is what you are working for. Once you reach the point of understanding that particular element, you can understand how it works within you, as well as what inspiration it brings to your life and how to fill any gaps you may perceive. If your perception of the element does not change over time, you may be in a stagnant mode and need to balance yourself by bringing in another element altogether or by working with elemental combinations for a while.

Forming a bond with an element can bring meaning to your spiritual practice on several levels. It can also increase your magical power. An Air Witch can conjure the wind, for example. In order to know how to work with air, she must study air and hold herself accountable to its honor. Each of the specialty paths holds the power of that element. Long ago, magical workers tried to control the elements, but that is not what this book is about. This book is about learning to work in harmony with a preferred element and individualizing your spiritual path with the element's life-affirming attributes. The elements cannot be controlled. Anything they decide to do on your behalf is their choice, so never take them for granted. They may do something for you once and then refuse to do it again. The powers they share with you are not to be abused.

Each element has special magical rites, deities, folklore, and fantasy creatures associated with it. There are also specific herbs, colors, and crystals that fall under the rule of each element.

Within Wiccan paths today, the elements are often seen as forces of nature with no personality or spirit within them. However, this is a common misperception.

Deity represents the elements and spirit as well. When deity is seen with a predominant elemental quality, this is a reflection of nature. Deity can be seen as an incarnation of spirit *within* nature. For example, there is Pele, the Hawaiian volcano goddess. Pele has all of the characteristics you would expect of fire. She is seen as the essence of fire. Hence, she is the embodiment of spirit within nature—as fire.

It is important to note that this book emphasizes the four elements of earth, air, fire, and water, and not the nature spirits known as elementals. Gnomes, sylphs, salamanders, and undines will be discussed, but when I say elemental force, I mean the element itself, not the nature spirit. Nature spirits exist for each element, and they can be tricky to work with. In truth, it takes years of hard work to gain even a small amount of knowledge about their perceptions of our world.

If you choose to work with the nature spirits, do your research first! It is easy to misunderstand their intentions and goals, and you may end up inadvertently offending them. They are of a realm that is completely different from ours. The elementals are considered to be soulless, and there are legends about both their kindness and their animosity. Certain types of nature spirits are not known for their fondness of humans. Use caution and respect when approaching any nature spirit, and always know which one you are dealing with.

Nature spirits entwine with the elements themselves. They occupy a different plane of existence, and there are many separate races of them. Our plane overlaps with theirs, just as all four elements overlap within our plane.

Choosing the path of an Air Witch, for example, does not mean that air is the *only* element you will be working with, just the main one. It goes without saying that spirit will be involved. In many of the Air Witch workings, you will see the presence of other elements involved as well. It is rare to find an element separate from the others within nature and impossible to separate an element from spirit.

Water may put out a fire, but it also evaporates in the sun, which is a representation of fire in nature. Water evaporates through the element of air and travels back to Earth as rain. All of the elements are tied to one another in various ways.

There has been much debate about the topics of the cardinal directions, placement of the Watchtowers, guardians, and corresponding elements. The correspondences presented here are my own. If you have a traditional set of correspondences that you prefer to stick with, by all means do so. Your level of comfort directly influences your spiritual path, so you should keep it at its highest level whenever possible.

When the elements combine forces, they produce tremendous power for us to draw from. Hurricanes, earthquakes, volcanic explosions, and the like are examples of combined elements. On the other side of the coin we find things like rainbows. Rainbows are gentle, but they require more than one element to be produced. We will discuss elemental combination specialties in the last chapter.

The elements come together in various ways in nature, and it is the same in the lives of Elemental Witches. The Earth is our foundation, the base on which we build. It is solid and strong. Water will pound and pound on it and shape it into new land masses. The way these two elements interact is similar to how Water Witches and Earth Witches interact. Air Witches have trouble grounding themselves, while Earth Witches can't seem to get off the ground. Each path teaches the other path. They need each other and the balance found therein. Element-based covens can help you maintain your balance, but if one is not available to you, simply remember to keep your balance. If you choose to work predominantly with one element, make sure you incorporate the other elements into your practice on a regular basis.

Element-based altars are simple to set up and are often quite beautiful. Please remember to include at least a small representation of the other elements as well, to maintain a balance. You may prefer to set up the altar with a focus on a particular element for when you work with that element, but keep it set up as equal and balanced the rest of the time.

The character sketches used in the elemental path chapters of this book have their basis in the elements themselves as well as traditional deities and ancient occult beliefs. All of the personality quirks of a particular Elemental Witch may not apply to you, but you should be able to identify with the composite enough to realize it's the most similar to you.

Once you think you have identified your elemental preference, try it on. How does it feel? Always go with your gut instinct. If it doesn't feel quite right, perhaps you should try another. This book can help you thoroughly explore the various paths and recognize any patterns that reveal an elemental preference. However, it cannot tell you how to feel about that preference. So even if you have all of the characteristics of fire (according to this book), if fire does not feel right yet air does, go with air. Also, health clues can be tricky. For example, I prefer to work with air, yet one of my health clues was the development of asthma. In my case, it served to show me how important air is to me, but at first glance you would think it ruled out air.

Are you ready to begin your journey and personalize your path? Good. Then turn the page and let's get started.

2

DISCOVERING YOUR
ELEMENTAL AFFINITY

This chapter is designed to help you find your elemental preferences. The tools included are a questionnaire, meditation exercises, and vision quest instructions. There are many clues in our daily lives that can serve to reveal to us any elemental affinities we may already have. We need only to look closely at ourselves and our situations to find them.

Our health and any related problems can offer insight into our elemental affinities. The Greeks based their medical system on the four elements. Hippocrates' theory was so sound that much of it is still in use today. His influence on medicine has lasted throughout the ages, as all doctors still take the Hippocratic oath. In ancient Greek medicine, each element corresponded to a bodily fluid, called a humour. It was thought that all diseases were caused by an imbalance of the elements in the patient. We can use Hippocrates' ideas to determine if an imbalance is present within us. For instance, I am an Air Witch with liver problems. This directly corresponds with the ancient belief that air rules the liver. A little research into this subject may be very revealing about what predominant element lives within you.

The ancient Cherokees based their system of natural medicine around the elements as well. Each plant corresponded to a specific direction, and the direction specified what type of medicine the plant was to be used for. The goal was to create and maintain a balance to ward off sickness.

According to the Cherokee medicine system, the direction of east corresponded to the element of fire and was related to family, fertility, and emotions. The direction of west corresponded to water and was used in matters of internal medicine. The direction of north corresponded to the element of air and was used in matters related to mental conditions and colds and airborne sicknesses. The direction of south corresponded to earth and was used in matters involving cuts, bruises, and external hurts.

WHICH ELEMENT ARE YOU?

You can gain insight into your personal elemental affinities by asking yourself questions that cover a wide range of topics. Ask yourself many simple questions. Think of it as peeling an onion. Layer by layer you slowly reveal your core. Revealing spells have their purposes, like when it comes to remembering things we may have chosen to forget, but when it comes to determining something as deeply ingrained as an elemental affinity, you must peel, peel, and peel. If you write your answers on a single sheet of paper, one element will often appear many times. Here is a list of questions to consider:

1. What element do you feel you align with?

2. List any hobbies you have. Is there a recurrent theme?

3. Are you basically happy and content or restless and bored?

4. How are you when it comes to money matters?

5. Do you have a sharp nose for business?

6. What are your favorite food groups or preferred taste sensations? (Sweet, salty, etc.)

7. Are you an artist? If so, what medium do you prefer? (Words, paint, sculpture, etc.)

8. What is your preferred divination method? (Tarot, scrying, pendulum, etc.)

9. Do you know your aura colors?

10. Do you have past-life memories?

11. What are your preferred textures? (Satin, cotton, etc.)

12. How would you describe your musical taste? What is your favorite type of music?

13. What is your favorite kind of mood enhancer? (Aroma, music, stones, etc.)

14. Do you have any physical impairments? (Hearing, sight, smell, etc.) Do you have asthma or any other type of health condition?

15. Do you have any phobias?

16. What is your favorite activity?

17. What is your preferred reading genre? (Fantasy, horror, nonfiction, etc.)

18. How old are you?

19. What kind of imagery do you prefer? (A waterfall, roaring fire, sky scene, luxuriant garden, etc.)

20. Do you collect anything?

21. What is your favorite color?

22. Do you have a weight problem? (Are you overweight or underweight?)

23. Tell me about your space . . . Is it organized or cluttered?

24. Do you have any bad habits?

25. What color is your car?

26. Do you follow the Wiccan Rede or the Golden Rule?

27. Do you believe in the threefold law?

28. Do you have an altar? What is on it?

29. Are your rituals formal or informal?

30. Tell me about your book of shadows. Is it organized? Divided into sections? How many sections? Are the pages decorated, or is it more of a journal? Tell me all about it.

31. How do you handle anger?

32. How do you handle love?

33. Are you methodical or more free-spirited?

34. What is your Sun sign? Moon sign? Ascendant?

35. What is your profession? What do you want it to be?

36. Do you believe in ghosts? What would you consider to be "proof" of a haunting?

37. Do you have a totem animal? If so, what is it?

38. Is there a season of the year that you feel most in tune with?

39. Do you consider yourself a day person or a night person?

40. What mythical or fantasy creatures do you love? Which ones scare you?

41. Looking in your book of shadows, what type of spells are predominant? (Candles, herbs, mojo bags, etc.)

42. What color are your eyes? Your hair?

43. Where are you most comfortable? (At home, in the forest, at the beach, etc.)

44. Do you have any specific dream memories? Describe them.

MEDITATION

Meditation is an effective way of uncovering deep-seated elemental influences. Even people who seem to have no elemental preference can often find one if they look deeply enough.

Each element offers particular lessons and insights into our world and the world beyond. You can meet the elements individually or all in one session. Before you choose a predominant element, I recommend that you first take the time to commune with that element and meet your elemental guide one-on-one.

To Meet Your Earth Guide

Set up a simple altar with a green or brown candle and herbal incense. You may wish to use a green altar cloth and your pentacle. Cast your personal circle. Take several slow, deep, cleansing breaths and relax your whole body. Close your eyes. Allow your breathing to slow and become regular. Take deep, slow breaths. Visualize the gateway to earth. Make the gate as elaborate as you wish, using any material that you desire. To open, does it swing wide? Does it lift up? Does it dissolve? Keep focused on your breath, and allow the gate to open. Relax. Walk through the gateway and down the path. Take a moment to observe the world around you. The grass is a beautiful emerald green. There are flowering trees and shrubs everywhere you look. The nearby hillsides are covered with flowers and green, healthy grass. As you walk, you notice a figure in the distance. Walk toward it. Stay focused on your breath. Standing in front of you is your guide for exploring the elemental realm of earth. It could be an animal, a human, or a mythical creature. Greet your guide. Listen to what he has to say. When you have heard all you wish, thank him. Always respect your guide, as he will be with you a long time. Slowly walk back up the pathway to the gate. Focus on your breath. Walk through the gate and see it close. Allow yourself a few more deep breaths and then open your eyes. Write down what you learned in a journal for safekeeping. Close your circle.

To Meet Your Air Guide

Create a simple altar with a yellow cloth, a blue candle, and an air type of incense. (Lavender or mint work very well.) You may wish to place feathers or a bell on the altar. Cast your personal circle. Take several deep, cleansing breaths. Close your eyes. Visualize the elemental gateway to the realm of air. Make the gate as elaborate as you wish. How does the gate open? Relax and focus on your breath. See the gate open, and walk through it. Before you is a pathway woven together out of fluffy white clouds. Begin to walk down the path. Take a few moments to observe the world around you. You can see clear skies to your right; they are a beautiful crystal blue. To your left you can see rumbling storm clouds in the distance, and lightning flashes inside of them. Continue on your way. In the distance you see a figure. It is your guide for the elemental realm of air. Walk to him. Focus on your breath. Greet your guide and listen to what he has to say. When you have heard all you wish, thank your guide. Begin to walk back to the gateway. Focus on your breath. Walk through the gateway and see it close. Take a few deep breaths and then open your eyes. Write down what you learned in your journal, and close your personal circle.

To Meet Your Water Guide

Create a simple altar with a bowl of water and floating blue candles. Use a rain-scented incense. You may keep a chalice filled with wine or a favorite herbal tea on the altar. Take several deep, cleansing breaths. Cast your personal circle. Close your eyes. Visualize the gateway to the elemental realm of water. What does it look like? How does it open? Focus on your breath. Keep your breathing deep, slow, and steady. See the gate open, and walk through it. Amazingly, you find yourself walking across the bottom of the sea, yet you can still breathe easily, encased in your own personal bubble. The sand is firm under your feet. Around you are bright coral shells, starfish, sea horses, and dolphins. Schools of brightly colored fish swim by. Walk slowly toward the figure you see in the distance. Focus on your breath. You are calm, relaxed, and happy. Greet your elemental guide for the realm of water, and listen to what he has to say. When you have heard all you wish, thank him. Begin to walk back toward the gateway. Stay focused on your breath as you take one last look at the beautiful world beneath the waves. Walk through the gateway and see it close. Take several deep breaths and then open your eyes slowly. Write down what you learned in your journal. Close your circle.

To Meet Your Fire Guide

Create a simple altar with an orange cloth and a red candle. Use an amber- or wood-scented incense. Take several deep, cleansing breaths. Get comfortable. Focus on your breathing, and close your eyes. Visualize the gateway to the elemental realm of fire. Make the gate as strong and elaborate as you wish. How does it open? Take several slow, deep breaths. See the gate open, and walk through it. Everything is dark. Before you is a pathway illuminated with candles on each side. It is a broad, safe pathway. Begin to walk down it. Slowly, stars become visible in the dark sky. Take a moment to appreciate the twinkling lights. Focus on the candle flames and note that no two are exactly alike. They dance in various colors on the tips of the candles. You feel warm, safe, and happy. Focus on your breath. Further on down the path you see your elemental guide for the realm of fire. Approach him slowly and greet him warmly. Listen to what he has to say. When you have heard all you wish, thank him and turn to go back up the path. As you approach the gateway, notice that it is still open. Walk through it. Take several slow, deep breaths and then open your eyes. Write down all you learned in your journal. Close your personal circle.

Opening the elemental gateways can allow you to learn more about the elements and the sacred knowledge they contain. When determining an elemental affinity, opening the gateway of an element allows you the confidence to be positive of your choice before aligning with the element. Also, once aligned, you still have the option to switch your focus to another element entirely, should you need to do so.

One way to open the elemental gateways is to meditate on the ancient symbols of the elements, or tattwas (see next page). The tattwas are symbols that are considered to be keys to the subconscious and collective conscious of the universe. The easiest way to put a tattwa to use is to stare at it, unblinking, until the image is burned into your mind. Then close your eyes, and, using the image held in your mind, your subconscious will open the gateway.

Opening the Gateways Simultaneously

After a suitable meditation time with the tattwas, when you feel you are ready, stand and face north. Visualize the northern gate with the tattwa of earth carved upon it. The entry can be a golden gateway or a monolithic stone structure, or even a simple wooden gate. Stare into the tattwa until its aura begins to become visible, then shift your focus to the gateway. You should begin to see the fog lift, and the portal

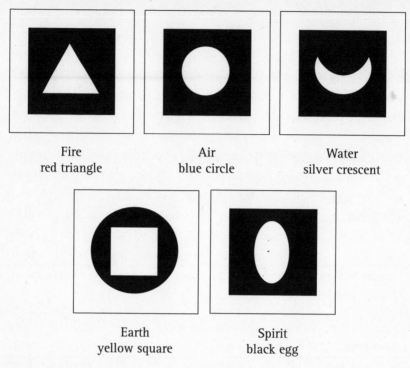

Fire	Air	Water
red triangle	blue circle	silver crescent

Earth
yellow square

Spirit
black egg

Tattwa Symbols

will become clear. It may look like a swirling vortex at first, but it will eventually take on a form that represents that element. Turn east and repeat the process. Continue with all four of the elements if you wish, or you may choose to open only one gateway at a time. If you wish, you may protect yourself with a personal bubble and enter into the realm of the element. Be sure to ask that the gate remain open. Explore and commune as long as you like. When you are done, make sure to close each gateway by allowing your vision to blur as you look at it. The vortex should become active again, and the fog will settle.

VISION QUESTING

A vision quest is no easy task to accomplish, but it will open your eyes to many things in this world that you had not noticed before. A vision quest pushes the body, mind, and soul to the extreme, where they all meet and come together. It is essential for all parts of ourselves to be in harmony with each other and with nature.

It is not necessary to do a full eight-day vision quest to discover your elemental affinity, but if you wish to you certainly can. I recommend the following quest, which is simpler and more harmonious to our roles in daily life. At this point, you should have some idea of which element you prefer.

1. Fast on juice and water for one day while you meditate and focus on your personal elemental characteristics.

2. Early the next morning, set out for a long walk. Plan to spend the whole day communing with nature. Take only water with you. If you can arrange to camp out for the night, so much the better. If not, spend at least an hour focusing on the Earth itself. Notice the differences in grass blades, dirt types, and tree barks.

3. Open up a dialog in your head with one of the elements, asking it all you wish to know. Do the same with the other three elements in turn.

4. Do not allow yourself to sleep that night, if possible. Spend it communing with the elements instead.

5. Keep an eye out for a sign, be it a hawk flying that catches your attention or a special star twinkling. Your personal element will reveal itself in a unique way.

6. When you return home, honor yourself and the element that came to you with a ritual. You do not have to dedicate yourself to a particular element in order to learn more about it. Simply ask that element to show you more, and remember to say thank you. Courtesy and respect go a long way.

7. Bless yourself with a simple statement of intent. Say something like, "I am blessed within the eyes of my Lord and Lady." Throughout this entire process, do not be afraid to cry and laugh. A successful vision quest is a highly charged emotional task and quite an accomplishment.

If it is possible for you to do a full eight-day vision quest, the process is more elaborate, as follows:

1. There is a three-day preparation period, during which you spend all of your time searching for your personal element by discussing your personality and viewpoints with the universe or whomever happens to be around. Every topic that pops into your mind is appropriate, so be sure to keep accurate notes. You swim to soak up water energy, practice breathing techniques to soak up air energy, lie on the ground to soak up earth energy, and allow the sun to shine on you to soak up fire energy. This time is meant to prepare you for your task.

2. For the next three days, go out into nature alone, with no food, only water. Fast, meditate, commune with the elements, and do a great amount of personal reflection. Stay out in the wild until you see your sign, your vision, of your personal element. On the fourth morning, you may return home. During this time period, you are allowed nothing that does not come from nature itself and no food. Physical activity is encouraged. If you see your sign before the fourth day, it is a personal choice whether to stay on the journey or to return home. Let your instincts guide your choice.

3. When you return home, hold a ceremony of rebirth, for you have been reborn into your element. Traditional Native American rites call for a sweat lodge cleansing, but this can also be done with smudging. To smudge yourself, light a smudging stick or burn sage on a charcoal tablet. Pass your arms through the smoke, then your legs, and so on, until you have exposed your whole body to the cleansing effect of the sage smoke After the cleansing, it's time to write your story.

4. Perform a rite of honor, such as a ritual bath with all the trappings.

If you have performed all of these steps and are still not sure which element is best to work with, study the four Elemental Witch path chapters and continue the meditations. Your element will eventually reveal itself; it just may choose to wait a bit until the time is right.

PART ONE
EARTH

3

THE PATH OF THE EARTH WITCH

The path of the Earth Witch most closely resembles that of a Kitchen Witch or a Green Witch. It is grounded in the home and family. Whether gardening, cooking, or cleaning, the Earth Witch brings magic into her life at its simplest level. She becomes one with the Earth. The Earth Witch accepts that everything she does is a reflection of the cycle in nature, down to the cell multiplications in her body, and she considers all of it to be magical. She fully understands the mysteries of the Earth.

In almost all religious traditions and mythologies, humans sprang forth from the Earth. The Earth allows us to draw energy from it and to return that energy to it. It cleanses us by its very presence. We may purge into the Earth any negative vibrations that bother us, and we can depend on it to do a thorough job of cleansing them away.

The Witch who follows the element of earth is similar to the Kitchen Witch in her use of herbs and magic in the kitchen as well as her affinity for "home-grown" magic and simple folk magic. The Earth Witch incorporates magic into the spice additions and stirring patterns of the majority of meals she prepares in her home.

The Earth Witch relates to the path of the Green Witch in that they both often are gardeners. It is not unusual to find Earth Witches with statues and beautiful rock formations in their gardens. They decorate them in much the same manner as they do their homes. Often, they tend their edible gardens the closest, while courting the favor of the gnomes to watch over their more delicate plants.

The Earth Witch views her home as an extension of the Earth in every way; it is like her own personal slice of the Earth. The kitchen is a direct extension of the garden and, therefore, of the Earth.

The Earth Witch specializes in protection magic, past-life discovery, prosperity, and fertility. She trains to hold herself closely to the honors of the Earth by recycling and practicing eco-magic. She often is very frugal and prefers to make the things that she can rather than buy them. She can usually make her own cleaning products, candles, and all types of herbal remedies. From healing teas to lice treatments, the Earth Witch understands that the magic is within the Earth itself and within her. She knows exactly which herb to prescribe to cheer you up or relax you. Herbs are her special course of study.

The Earth Witch lives in a world where every knife is a potential athame and every glass a chalice. While she does perform more formal rituals, for the most part she keeps things informal and constant. She holds her path close to her heart and has no illusions about how grand magic can be. She knows that it takes work. She is grounded in reality.

The Earth Witch views spirit as a part of her and everything she does. She accepts that spirit lives within everything in existence. Because her view of spirit is so all-encompassing, she understands that not all things have rational explanations. However, she is the first to try to find a scientific explanation before chalking up an experience to something "supernatural." While she easily accepts the existence of spiritual conjurations and the like, she does not do so blindly. She keeps her mind open.

Though the Earth Witch is often perceived as boring or a homebody, she stands on a foundation that is unshakable. If you are friends with an Earth Witch, you have a true friend. She has a very nurturing and protective quality and is loyal and dependable.

The home of an Earth Witch is lived-in, comfortable, happy, and usually well organized—she runs a tight ship. At the same time, the Earth Witch is the first to let housework slide a bit. Her view is that as long as everything is in its place, a little dust is okay. She recognizes that many times there are more important things to do than mindless scrubbing. It is not unusual for an Earth Witch to incorporate magical correspondences into her décor. She usually has an abundance of house plants and tends to have a green thumb when it comes to the care of these plants.

The kitchen is by far the most popular room in the Earth Witch's house. She considers it to be the heart of her home—and her home is her heart. The aromas drifting from the kitchen tend to make folks gravitate into the room. The Earth Witch appreciates good cooking. She is renowned for her ability to whip up a meal from scratch while visiting with others. Unfortunately, due to this love, she also may have issues with weight and carry a few extra pounds.

While taste is important to the Earth Witch, texture is even more important. The Earth Witch is sensual and loves touching and being touched. She may have an affinity to velvet, silk, and more exotic fabrics, but you will most often find her dressed in comfortable cotton. She has a strong affinity to stones and crystals and often wears them as jewelry.

The Earth Witch understands the forces at work behind crystal energy. She knows that crystals contain electrical charges and can be used as batteries, both personally and in electronic devices. She is usually well versed in magnetic magic as well.

The Earth Witch's book of shadows is often painstakingly kept. Thorough and detailed, it can contain entire family histories within its pages. It is usually scrupulously organized and filled with any fact that could possibly be needed. The Earth Witch treasures family heirlooms and creates her personal book of shadows in such a way that it will stand the test of time. To her, it is not only a book of magic, it is a manual of life, and it is meant to be passed down through the family.

One of the best things about the Earth Witch is her ability to remain silent. She understands that sometimes it is best to say nothing rather than risk saying it wrong. She is very careful about what she says. Because she is not argumentative by nature, when the Earth Witch speaks, her words hold weight. She also tends to be critical of others, even though she may not say it out loud. Too often, the Earth Witch represses her feelings and as a result may need to purge more often than those who follow other elemental paths. But since she holds earth so close, she is adept at purging anywhere and anytime.

Cautious and wary, the Earth Witch rarely takes unnecessary chances. Level-headed to the end, she helps others find suitable solutions to their problems. Her approach to life is slow and steady. She is conservative, patient, and practical.

The Earth Witch can most often be found working a job in which she can directly improve the world around her, or a job that may seem boring but is traditionally necessary within the boundaries of society. Social work, teaching, architecture, and banking are natural choices for the Earth Witch.

On the flip side, the gentle Earth Witch is not one you want to anger. She is capable of utter destruction, which she views as a natural part of the cycle of life. Rarely will she look back with regret. She may take a while before deciding that she is angry and will give you every chance to explain yourself. But once angered, she can be stubborn and hold a grudge. Because she will give you every chance in the beginning, if she decides that she doesn't like you—well, you earned it. Most people only get to cross that line once with an Earth Witch. However, she is eternally forgiving toward those she loves and trusts.

Because the Earth Witch is so rooted to the home, she must be careful not to shut herself away from others entirely. However, she is rarely shy and can often be found at social gatherings.

The Earth Witch may have a talent for sculpting, even if she doesn't know it yet. When holding chunks of clay in her hands, she can create some beautiful statuary. Clay falls in her natural realm of elemental attributes.

The Earth Witch is a teacher and strives to set a good example for her students, children, and friends. She practices what she preaches and believes that actions speak louder than words. For thousands of years, the bones of the Earth (rocks) have been utilized as teaching implements. Pictographs (painted-on symbols) and petroglyphs (carved symbols) date back to the ancient Egyptians. Almost every culture has its own version of rock teachings.

Earth rules the season of spring. During the spring, the Earth and the Earth Witch come roaring back to life. As the flowers bloom, the grass grows, and the animals wake from their slumber, the Earth Witch becomes one with all of nature. She is directly influenced by the increasing life energy of all things. Her personal power is at its highest point during this season.

One of the most prevalent aspects of the path of the Earth Witch is sharing. Mother Earth shares all of herself with the other elements. She allows herself to be the foundation for all of life. She is battered by storms and ravaged by fire, but she remains unchanged yet ever evolving. The Earth Witch holds herself close to this archetype. She struggles to remain calm and steady during all of life's storms. She has a unique talent for being able to keep her cool. She also has the minor quirk of being slow to movement. The Earth is constantly moving, but it is imperceptible to humans. The Earth Witch knows that she has all the time in the world—she is not the sort to jump around and do things right away. "All in good time" is her motto. However, she must be extremely careful with this aspect of her personality, as it can cause her to stagnate and stop her growth. As a rule, the Earth Witch resists change.

When it comes to divination practices, the Earth Witch can read better by scrying into water or fire than by using the divination systems that fall under the rule of earth. This is because of her role as the base for the other elements. The Earth as a whole contains water and fire and serves as a foundation for air. There is much more to the Earth than dirt and plant life.

Humanity belongs to the realm of earth. Any type of folk magic that utilizes footprints, hair or nail clippings, etc., is an Earth Witch's specialty.

The Earth Witch is a puzzle of Hoodoo, Voodoo, Native American beliefs, shamanistic behaviors, Wiccan ethics (or the Golden Rule), and/or ancestral lore. Yet she is a puzzle in which all of the pieces fall in place to create a beautiful picture.

THE DARK SIDE OF THE EARTH WITCH

All beings have their strengths and weaknesses. In the case of an Earth Witch, there is one main magical problem: she has a hard time defending herself against things that are "unearthly." Spiritual entities or adverse astral conditions are rare occurrences, but since they force the Earth Witch out of her natural realm, they can cause quite a bit of stress and wreak havoc. Because these entities have an easier time attacking the Earth Witch, they tend to do so more often than they do the other Elemental Witches. Because of this problem, the Earth Witch is usually very practiced in warding and protection. This is also a prime argument for maintaining balance in one's magical practice. Each element has its own set of strengths and weaknesses. Where one element may have a hole, another may fill it with energy.

However, the enterprising Earth Witch has (and has had for centuries) the perfect tool to remedy this problem: the bridge. Crossing running water serves to release her from any hounding spirits. In order for an Earth Witch to fight unearthly forces effectively, she must call upon her sister elements. It is in this capacity that her role of being the foundation of life is of the greatest importance. Her ability to draw from her sister elements and seek their aid becomes more pronounced each time she does it. Practice makes perfect for an Earth Witch.

It is important to note that an Earth Witch can have a hard time understanding her sister elements. In truth, all practitioners of specialty paths have to find their own unique ways of relating to those who follow a different elemental path. The Earth Witch is both battered and pampered by the other elements. For example, a hurricane-force wind may change the surface of the Earth, but it cannot change the core of it. The Earth Witch is the same. She can adapt to the wind on the surface, but it does not change who she is or her role in the world.

EARTH WITCH LORE

Caves

Most caves have local folklore surrounding them, with one common theme: they are inhabited by spirits or dragons and are forbidding places, desolate and dank. So many legends tell of ghosts haunting caves. These legends were perpetuated by pirates and the like to scare people away from their hiding places and thereby keep their loot hidden. They also stem from ancient days when bears and lions might be found in the caves.

For ages, the members of ancient tribes lived their entire lives in caves. In Sweetwater, Tennessee, there is a cavern known as "the Lost Sea," which features an underground lake with its own variety of plant life (which only grows underground). It is said to be the home of the white jaguar. This cavern is a world within the world. The hauntingly beautiful columns of stalagmite drip healing waters upon those who stand beneath it. Not surprisingly, this cave is also thought to be haunted. It was sacred to the Cherokee tribes.

The Earth Witch knows and understands that caves actually relate to the process of birth. Spirit haunts a cave as a "pregnancy," or a continuation of life. Therefore, a cave is sacred ground. All that it holds within relates to life and death, as it all stems from the cave. The cave is the birth canal of Mother Earth.

Bridges

Rivers belong to the Water Witch, but bridges, and the superstitions that surround them, belong to the Earth Witch. As one who finds solutions and builds foundations, who else could conceive of a way to cross running water while remaining earthbound?

There are a few mythical bridges that relate to other elements, such as Bifrost (the rainbow bridge leading from Midgard, the realm of the mortals, to Asgard, the realm of the gods, in Norse mythology), but more often bridges belong to the realm of earth.

A bridge is a gateway, because it rests between two bodies of land mass. While crossing it, you are neither in one space nor the other. The bridge transcends the two objects it connects in this manner; hence, it is a very magical and powerful place. It has been said that time does not work the same way on bridges as it does elsewhere. Some say that time moves more slowly when on a bridge, while others say that time ceases to exist all together and does not begin again until one has crossed completely over. Because of the time factor, a bridge has the ability to bring one back to a childlike state.

In many myths, a bridge is the path one must take after death to reach the other side. Some of the mythical bridges were treacherous, in order to keep out the living. Native American lore speaks of a shaking bridge one must cross to reach the other side. Often these mythical bridges are said to not tolerate the weight of a sinner and will cast the sinner off the bridge into the water below.

There is a tale in modern folklore that relates that you will hear a heartbeat if you stand quietly on a bridge. I have heard about a million variations of this urban legend with one common theme: that of the heartbeat belonging to a deceased person. While it is possible to hear a heartbeat-type noise on certain bridges throughout the United States, this is normally due to nearby gas pipes or some other human invention. Yet the tale lives on because of the spooky reputation of bridges.

Because of the association with death, bridges are often said to be haunted. Celtic tradition warns that you should hold your tongue while crossing or passing beneath a bridge. The Isle of Man is home to the famed Fairy Bridge. Local legend says that if you cross the bridge without wishing the little people that live there a good day, you will not have a safe or happy visit. There is also a universal belief that two people who part on a bridge will never meet again.

Earth Witches know the lore to be true to this point—there is magic aplenty contained in the bridge. Spell work performed on a bridge tends to take effect immediately. Any type of magic that involves time manipulation will gain a boost by being performed on a bridge.

Trolls

Trolls, or trows as they are sometimes called, are often thought to live under bridges. They are said to be ugly little creatures, but there are some old myths that claim that trows could pass for human. Some of the myths infer that trows are nocturnal and can only move about at night, while others say they are invisible and therefore simply unseen. Folklore from the Shetland Islands in Scotland lays claim to one distinguishing character trait carried by trolls: they walk backwards. Trolls have a distinct hatred for locked doors and are known to sneak into people's homes at night if the occupants have locked the door before retiring.

While the tales of the troll featured in folklore contain both gruesome and nonsensical elements, there is little doubt that the troll relates to and falls under the rule of earth. Trolls were known to have magical powers. It was said that they could fly and enchant the wind and were masters of mixing healing potions, ointments, and elixirs.

Sacred Circles

Everything from crop circles to stone circles belongs to the realm of the Earth Witch.

Salisbury Plain, in southern England, boasts the ownership of the megalithic ruins known as Stonehenge. Similar ruins dot the European continent in well over five hundred places. Carbon dating has revealed that Stonehenge is four thousand years old. The tallest stone is over twenty-two feet high, with another eight feet buried beneath the ground. Each stone is said to weigh around twenty-five tons.

Archeologists have argued for ages as to the purpose of Stonehenge. Some assert that Stonehenge was built by the Druids as a place of worship. We will probably never know for certain if Stonehenge was indeed built by the ancient Druids, but the link between Stonehenge and today's Druids is certainly real. They frequently hold rituals and meetings there.

Stonehenge is perhaps the best-known example of an ancient stone circle, but lesser-known stone circles are found all over the Earth.

In West Africa, on the north bank of the river Gambia, there is a large collection of ancient stone circles—over one hundred of them. In N'jai Kunda, there is an example of an impressive standing stone circle in which the stones all weigh approximately ten tons each.

The stone circles in the Arctic region are a bit different than those at places like Stonehenge. In parts of Alaska, the landscape is covered with stones that form perfect circles. These were, at one time, thought to be some sort of ancient mystical force at work, but in reality their shape is owed strictly to nature. The constant freezing and thawing of the land results in an almost labyrinth type of landscape, and the stones fall into natural circular patterns. In other parts of the United States, there are wheels. Circular formations of stones, similar to those found in the Arctic region, are fairly prevalent in certain parts of the country. Big Horn Medicine Wheel, which sits on Medicine Mountain, Wyoming, is one of the best-known wheel formations.

Stone circles in ancient culture probably held their own significance. To the modern practitioner, they are virtual vortexes of energy. Standing stones magnify magical vibrations, and when formed in a circle, the barrier is impenetrable, allowing the magic to reach its full potential. It is a common practice in spell work to ring candles with stones or to make a circle boundary from stones when it is cast. Ringing an area or object with stones imparts all of the energies of those stones to the tool or person inside the circle. Modern Earth Witches hold this particular bit of information in high regard, as they are often seen wearing stone necklaces.

Crop circles, which burst onto the news scene close to twenty-five years ago, are areas in fields where the grass or grains have been leveled flat to form patterns. It is said that these circles appear overnight, close to dawn. It is further argued that these elaborate "circles" appear fully formed in some sixty seconds or less. While many of these circles have been revealed to be hoaxes (generally through found footprints or some other human evidence), there are accounts of genuine crop circles.

The true crop circles have strange effects on the world around them. Battery-powered objects and electrical equipment that work directly outside of the circle will not work within the circle's boundaries. The batteries are quickly drained. Radioactivity has been found in the soil in a very few cases, but electrical magnetic frequencies in the soil is a fairly common occurrence.

In some cases the crop undergoes a genetic mutation. The stalks that were pressed flat begin to experience a change within their cellular construction. Moreover, a genuine crop circle often features pressed stalks that have not been broken in any way. It is said that the effect is akin to the stalk being steamed and going limp.

Though crop circle research has been conducted primarily in southern England, crop circles have appeared all over the world. In Japan, a circle appeared in a rice paddy, and thousands of gallons of water disappeared. In Afghanistan, a Celtic cross–type of formation appeared in a snow-covered field. No footprints were found and no explanation has been offered. The primary seasons in which crop circles appear are spring and summer, so a winter snow formation is rare.

Another natural sacred-circle formation on Earth is the fairy ring. Fairy rings are circular-shaped areas in fields where the grass is either darker or worn down. Accounts of fairy rings have been in existence for several hundred years. The earliest recorded account is from the year 1590. In it, a witness describes a troop of fairies dancing in a circle where the ring was later found. In France, one fairy ring is reported to be a half mile in diameter and over seven hundred years old.

Old folklore states that if a human enters a fairy ring, he will be forced to join in the dance. While it will seem to be only minutes to him, the actual time he will remain enchanted will be three to seven years.

As with crop circles, the primary seasons for fairy rings are the spring and summer. Experts commonly agree that a fungus causes fairy rings to appear. Quite often, mushrooms appear in fairy ring formations.

Crop circles and fairy rings have another thing in common: eyewitnesses say that both are caused by whirlwinds.

Mountains and Mounds

Legendary mountains and mounds fall within the domain of the Earth Witch. While mountains are natural formations, mounds are human-made. Both are considered sacred space. The prevailing argument as to the purpose of the mounds is that they are sacred burial grounds.

The Navajos have an old legend that describes the creation of the six sacred mountains. The First Man and First Woman formed the mountains from a bag of dirt that they carried with them from the third world (spirit realm). They sent Turquoise Boy to one mountain, Abalone Shell Boy to another, Jet Boy to another, and White Bead Boy to another. The mountains were not satisfied with that arrangement and would rumble loudly with displeasure. Only two of the six mountains were happy. First Man and First Woman sent the beautiful Mixed Stones Boy and Girl to those mountains. They then sent the rest of the holy ones, including Grasshopper Girl and Yellow Corn Girl, into the mountains.

First Man and First Woman then fastened the mountains to the land with lightning bolts, stone knives, and sunbeams. They decorated them with shells, eggs, mists, and rain. They then blessed the mountains with chants and prayers. They believe that keeping the land beautiful pleases the ancestors, and pleasing the ancestors makes for a happy tribe.

The Earth Witch agrees with this philosophy. She makes regular use of eco-magic and often gets involved with environmental issues. She understands the true beauty and blessings of the Earth and does not take them for granted. She considers keeping the land clean a sacred responsibility.

Earth Spirits: Gnomes, Elves, Dwarves, and Leprechauns

I recommend approaching earth spirits with caution. They are of the elemental race and inhabit a completely different realm, so it is hard to impossible for a human to understand how their minds truly work.

Gnome statues in the garden add a touch of whimsy to the décor, but the legend behind their popularity is quite intriguing. It was said that a single ray of sunshine would turn a dwarf to stone. Somehow, this myth crossed with information about gnomes, and the trendy garden gnome statues came to be. Since gnomes are considered helpful to one's garden, placing gnome statues there is tradition in a well-tended garden.

Gnomes are actually a dwarfish race of earth spirits. They are the guardians of the hidden treasures of the Earth. Some legends maintain that they can be playful and mischievous and love to pull pranks on unsuspecting humans.

Elves were originally considered to be of a small stature as well. They were thought to be fairly playful and helpful. The legends of elves run the gamut from Santa's toy-making helpers to the more romantic portrayal popularized by the writings of J.R.R. Tolkien.

Dwarves are said to be the possessors of two types of magical stones: one that will make the owner invisible and one that will grant the owner great strength. Dwarves were well-known in Norse myths for their wisdom. On at least one occasion the gods themselves went to the dwarves for aid, due to their cleverness.

Leprechauns are known to be tricksters, because greedy humans are always trying to get their legendary pots of gold. Leprechauns are Irish in origin and are thought to be cobblers.

Crossroads

Crossroads are considered sacred in almost all magical traditions. A crossroads is a universally accepted place to hold rituals, leave offerings, or dispose of items you wish to be rid of. While this is not a natural creation but one that is humanmade, it still falls in the realm of earth.

It is believed that Hecate rules over the three-way crossroads. She can see the past, present, and future. It is said that if you should approach a three-way crossroads at night, you would hear her black dogs howling. Her altars have been erected at such places for centuries.

The four-way crossroads are considered to be powerful because all four directions meet at one point. Dirt, rocks, and sticks gathered from such a crossroads are said to have powerful spiritual connections, albeit tricky ones to master. In Greek myths, Oedipus met his fate at the crossroads. From the Yoruban people we have Legba (a god known for his clever tricks) ruling the crossroads.

Ancient people were afraid of what it meant when one direction met another direction. All manner of folklore is available concerning the crossroads. Fairies are said to hang about there, along with ghouls and goblins. Even the Christian Satan is said to roam the crossroads.

Earth Witches know that a crossroads is actually a place of sacred transformations, manmade or not. Frequently they see them as a metaphor for transformational points in our lives. In such a capacity, the crossroads relate to time.

EARTH MAGIC

The term "earth magic" is somewhat of a misnomer. Many of the magical techniques presented here do not utilize actual earth (dirt, etc.); however, they are typically considered to be earth specialties. Business, protection, prosperity, and fertility all fall in this category.

Earth magic utilizes two main techniques: burying and transporting. We transport basically anytime we use earth in a spell that does not include the burial of the item or take place directly upon the soil. For example, if a loved one tracked muddy footprints into my home and I swept them up and saved the dirt for later use in a healing spell, this would be considered transporting.

You may bury things in the earth for the purpose of cleansing an item of negative vibrations, ridding yourself of an item (banishing), planting seeds for future growth of crops, or blessing an item.

You may transport the element of earth by placing soil in a charm bag or in your home, using a mud mask, or even growing houseplants. Many magical practitioners make use of dirt by piling it on their altar and burning candles in the pile. As dirt is sacred, it is fine to do this.

Although traditions vary, and many practitioners prefer to keep their altar surface spotlessly clean, the Earth Witch uses the power of dirt.

It doesn't matter which of the techniques you use—burying and transporting both hold the full power of earth, even when the soil is used in small amounts.

Various kinds of dirt are said to perform specific functions in many magical practices. According to Hoodoo and Voodoo traditions, graveyard dirt is thought to hold within it the vibrations of the departed soul. The ritual collection of graveyard dirt includes getting in touch with the spirit of the body in the grave and leaving a payment for the dirt (usually a coin on the gravestone). For instance, if your intention was to use the dirt to cause harm, you would find a grave that held a murder victim or some other tragic soul and use the dirt from it. Also incorporated into the ritual collection of graveyard dirt is the time of day in which the dirt is collected and the corresponding area of the body in the grave. In other words, for a love spell, you would take dirt from the area where the heart of the body lies.

Dirt from a crossroads is considered sacred in almost all magical traditions. It is believed to be loaded with supernatural powers. It is used for protection, blessings, banishing, domination—virtually any purpose. It is thought to be neutral, so one has only to direct it according to one's wishes.

Santería incorporates the magical qualities of dirt in the following ways:

Bank dirt: Dirt from the area around a bank is thought to hold prosperity within it.

Courthouse dirt: Dirt from the area around a courthouse is used to gain victory in legal disputes.

Dirt from the bottom of a person's shoes: This dirt is said to allow one to dominate or cause harm to the owner of the shoes.

Dirt from the four corners: This mixture of dirt is thought to open the road to success. This particular dirt is considered a four-way crossroads.

Forest dirt: Forest dirt is considered protective.

Library dirt: Dirt from the area around a library is used in spells to increase one's knowledge and wisdom.

Mountain dirt: Dirt from a mountain is used in cleansing practices.

Racetrack dirt: This dirt is used in gambling spells to increase luck.

Seashore dirt: This dirt is thought to be cleansing.

THE IMPORTANCE OF SALT

Salt is a primary tool of any Witch, regardless of the personal path. It is a representation of earth in a mineral form. Salt is used in traditional magical practices for blessing, grounding, protection, and cleansing. It is frequently used as a base for other ingredients in powders, floor washes, bathing spells, and charm bags. Salt is seen as a feminine, nurturing mineral, whereas sulphur is thought to be the male, destructive mineral. Salt works in banishing spells by breaking up or splitting apart any negative influences, due to its purity. It is used in holy water and is a staple on most altars.

MAGICAL GARDENING

Magical and healing herb gardens are sanctuaries of the soul. Indeed, any garden is a magical one to the Witch.

The earliest formal record of gardening dates back to a stone tablet from Mesopotamia circa 4000 BC. It describes how Enki, the Sumerian god of water, provided fresh water to the dry land and thereby produced fruit trees and fields from a desertlike land. By 2250 B.C., the famed Hanging Gardens of Babylon were well established in the capital of Sumeria. These are considered to be the forerunners of gardens today.

In ancient Persia (modern-day Iraq), gardens were the playground of life. They served as a place of solace, a gathering place for friends and family, and a formal extension of the home outdoors. These gardens were called "Paradise" and were thought to be an Earthly view of what heaven must be like. They were cultivated carefully and tended to lovingly. Due to the desert conditions of the area, the gardens were usually enclosed by high walls. Many had aqueducts installed to maintain the irrigation needed for the gardens to thrive. Most often these gardens were formed into a square pattern and further divided into four smaller squares. Fountains and water channels were an important part of the architecture of the gardens. The gardens were said to have two of every fruit tree and plenty of places for sitting, so that one could rest and enjoy the view.

Zen gardening is considered an art form by many. A Zen garden is a dry-landscape style of garden consisting of sand trails raked into intricate patterns. Often, the trails are not made of sand at all but rather of a crushed type of granite, a very fine gravel. Many times the gravel pathways circle a rock or bush. The purpose of Zen gardening (the raking of the gravels) is to provoke contemplation and meditation. These gardens are thought to be very peaceful and restful to the eyes.

Traditional Japanese gardens invoke a sense of peace and tranquility in both the gardener and the person lucky enough to view the garden. According to the principles of Japanese gardening, each element introduced must be something that could occur naturally. For example, you can find a waterfall in nature, but not a fountain. Hence, a fountain has no place in a traditional Japanese garden.

Knot gardens are by far one of the most fantastical types of magical gardens. They can weave a spell right into the landscape. A knot garden is a very formal, precise arrangement of plants and trees. To create a magical knot garden, choose an herb that corresponds to your intent and plant it in a pattern. The pattern can be as intricate or a simple as you wish. It can be a symbol, meant to reaffirm the spell, or any pattern that you like.

The ancient Romans brought their gardens inside the home and invented the atrium. Many times the atrium was placed in the center of the home. The area was left roofless and was usually surrounded by walkways. It may have held reflecting pools, herbal gardens, and fruit trees.

One of today's most popular magical-gardening practices is moon gardening. This technique uses an ancient system of moon phases and astrological placements to calculate planting and harvesting times. In a moon garden, white and night-blooming flowers are the main ornaments.

A SEED BLESSING

When you must start a plant from seeds, it is proper to bless the seeds beforehand. Place them on your altar and light a white candle. Add a clear quartz crystal to the altar for extra energy. Say something like, "Lord and Lady, I ask that you bless these seeds and impart your energies into them so that a large, beautiful, strong plant may grow in your honor. So mote it be!" As you can see, the blessing need not be stiff or formal. A simple stated request works best.

Another way to bless the seeds is to call upon the universal energies of the elements. A simply stated request is usually enough.

A GARDEN DEDICATION

A special god or goddess garden can be a wonderful addition to your landscaping, with a small amount of planning. As an example, we will look at a garden dedicated to Hecate. Hecate is the ruler of the three-way crossroads, so if it is possible to place her garden close to one, it would be a smart choice. Traditionally, altars dedicated to Hecate were erected at such locations. For plant choices, look up her history and choose plants that have a symbolic connection to her, such as the poppy flower, azalea bush, and cypress tree. For decoration, a lantern is a good choice, as Hecate is said to always carry a torch and to be the embodiment of a living flame. A statue is always a wise choice as well.

In your overall landscaping, you can place a small tribute garden to Hecate where the paths meet in a three way-crossroads, if you have no actual roads near your garden. This is probably the safer choice to avoid toxic fumes from vehicles bothering your delicate plants.

Once the planting is complete, it is time to dedicate the garden. If you included any sort of altar component in your design, simply set it up for use. If you didn't, you can erect a temporary altar from a garden bench or large stone. If you can plan your planting schedule around the moon phases, so much the better. The dedication ritual should ideally be performed under a full moon.

Supplies

A chalice, filled with a sweet red wine
Several sticks of willow or sandalwood incense
4 clear quartz crystals, programmed with growth and love

Go around the garden and place the incense sticks in the ground. Light them and blow out the flames so that they begin to smoke. Once the aroma begins to drift through the gardens, say something along the lines of, "This smoke consecrates this garden as sacred ground. Only love and light may enter here."

Next, take the crystals and bury them at the cardinal points while calling upon the universal energies of each direction to aid your garden in its task to thrive. Be specific and ask each direction to bless the garden and leave behind some of its essence. *Important note:* You are not calling the corners per se, so a dismissal is not mandatory. However, if you feel you should include one, by all means do so.

Now, walk the circle with the chalice in hand, and splash the wine about the garden. Say, "I dedicate this land and all it contains to Hecate. Blessed it shall be. May it thrive and hold fast to her honor. As it is sacred ground, no one may pollute it. Hecate, come and dwell in your sanctuary!" Clap your hands three times. The dedication is now complete.

Tend this garden faithfully, but allow for nature to run its course. Hecate may have plans to add a plant here and there, and this should be allowed. However, you should remove any weeds (especially those that are not related to Hecate) and, if necessary, water the ground. Accept the notion that Hecate will reside with you as long as this area is maintained properly.

You can create a generic goddess garden by following the basic outline of a moon garden. Moon gardens frequently include all the silvery herbs as opposed to the greener varieties. They often feature gazing globes, wind chimes, white stones for pathways, and white stone benches for relaxing. Moon gardens offer delightful scents, as most of the flowers are very aromatic.

If you decide to incorporate lighting into a moon-garden design, keep it subtle and stick to pathways only. You want the moonlight to reflect off of the white and silvery plants, creating a glow. *Important note*: When sitting in a moon garden at night, it is not unusual to be attacked by insects. Prepare yourself beforehand with a solution of mint essential oil diluted in rubbing alcohol.

TREE MAGIC

Since the time of the ancient Druids, trees have been an important resource of the Earth. While they are valuable in monetary ways, they have a decidedly more spiritual history. Trees are believed to have wise spirits residing within them, and forests and groves are considered sacred places of worship.

While not every type of tree possesses the elemental attributes of earth, the practice of tree magic is a natural for the Earth Witch. She draws much of her strength from the spirits of the plant kingdom, of which trees are the largest members.

The most common methods for performing tree magic are simple to do, yet pack a powerful magical punch. To incorporate the magic of trees into your practice, you can:

1. Soak up the energy of the tree by sitting beneath it.
2. Mark symbols on the leaves and ask the tree for help.
3. Tie items onto the branches.
4. Carry a bit of the wood with you.
5. Make use of a corresponding wood in spell work.
6. Bury things at the root of the tree.

There are many old spells that direct one to harm the tree by stripping bark from it, driving nails into it, and breaking off branches. Please do not do any of these things, and always talk to your chosen tree before trying to use it for a magical purpose. It will often gift you with a branch or bark—if you remember to ask first.

The magical properties of trees are as follows:

Apple: Healing, love, honor, youth

Beech: Goals, strength, wisdom

Birch: Protection, purification

Cedar: Prosperity

Cypress: Protection, past-life regression

Elder: Healing, protection, prosperity

Elm: Protection

Fig: Fertility, strength, energy, health

Hawthorn: Love, protection, cleansing

Hazel: Protection, reconciling

Hickory: Endurance, strength

Juniper: Protection

Maple: Love, divination

Oak: Healing, strength, prosperity

Olive: Peace, security, fidelity

Palm: Strength, abundance

Pecan: Prosperity

Pine: Purification, health, prosperity, spiritual growth

Rowan: Protection, strength

Walnut: Healing, protection

Willow: Healing, protection, wishes, enchantments, gracefulness

AN EARTH WAND

For an earth-oriented magical wand, it is best to use a fallen branch from a maple, ash, or rowan tree. Take the branch, strip the bark, and lightly sand the surface. Carve the alchemical symbol for earth ($\triangledown$) into it. Add any other personal carvings you like. Use a malachite stone for the tip. Anoint the wand with cypress oil and bless it under a full moon. Allow it to charge under the moon all night. When not in use, store it in a green silk wrapping cloth to which you have added a teaspoon of dirt.

EARTH CHARMS

Some naturally occurring objects are said to be empowered with extra luck or magical powers. Those that fall in the realm of earth include four-leaf clovers, petrified wood, and fairy stones.

Four-Leaf Clovers

It is rare to actually find a four-leaf clover. It is universally accepted as an harbinger of good luck to come your way. This belief stems back to the ancient Druids and is Celtic in origin.

Petrified Wood

If you are lucky enough to find a piece of petrified wood, then you are lucky indeed. It holds the magical properties of secrets, wisdom, strength, and transformation. Pay special attention to your dreams after finding a piece of petrified wood, as the spirit of the tree may be trying to speak with you.

Fairy Stones

Fairy stones form a natural solar-cross shape. They are known as staurolite. These little stone charms contain vast reservoirs of power and are wonderful when it comes to helping you maintain balance within your chosen elemental specialty.

MAGICAL POWDERS

The making of a magical powder falls in the realm of earth, due to its dry form. If the ingredients are especially aromatic, the powder will incorporate the element of air, but as a rule it belongs primarily to earth.

Magical powders consist of a variety of ingredients. Everything from chalk to eggshells to herbs are placed in a mortar and ground to a fine powder. The powder is then sprinkled inside a charm bag or around an altar, burned in a censer, or even dissolved into a glass of liquid for drinking.

Connect To Earth Powder (for Grounding)

  1 teaspoon dirt from your yard or a favored plant

  3 drops patchouli oil

  1 teaspoon barley, wheat, corn meal, or rye

Combine the ingredients in a mortar, and grind to a fine powder. Sprinkle it about your meditation area to connect with earth while meditating. If you have trouble grounding after ritual or spell work, keep a bit in a covered box and smell it or touch it when you need help grounding.

Protection Powder

  Basil

  Salt

  Garlic

  1 piece white chalk

Grind like amounts of all the ingredients together with a mortar and pestle in a clockwise pattern. Continue until the mixture is a fine powder. Open your third eye, and see the powder turn a glowing light purple. Bless it and empower it by saying, "Mother blesses my home with protection and safety. All here stay healthy, happy, and whole. As I speak it, so mote it be!"

You may go a step further and charge the powder under a full moon, if you'd like, but it is fine to use it right away. Walk around your house clockwise three times while sprinkling it onto the ground. Now your home is protected.

Lust Dust

  Orange zest

  Damiana

  Catnip

Hibiscus

Lavender

3 drops vanilla extract

1 drop musk oil (synthetic)

Grind like amounts of the first five ingredients in your mortar and grind to a fine powder. Add the vanilla extract and musk oil. Once the liquid is fully absorbed, grind a little more. Empower the mixture with a chant. Compose a simple, direct sentence of what you expect the lust dust to do, and use it as a chant. Sprinkle the dust about the bedroom or wherever you want the seduction to take place. Lust dust works extremely well (and quickly) when loaded into magenta candles.

Happy Home Powder

1 eggshell

Pinch of dirt from your garden or a favored plant

Rosemary

Petals from a white rose

Salt

Combine the eggshell, dirt, and equal amounts of rosemary, white rose petals, and salt in a mortar and pestle, and grind to a fine powder in a clockwise motion. Empower and sprinkle it in the corners of each room.

EDIBLE EARTH

Earth Bread Crescent Cakes

This recipe is a proper replacement for traditional almond crescent cakes in the cake and ale ceremonies. This bread relates closely to earth and is a good grounding aid.

$1/3$ cup butter

$2^1/4$ cups flour

4 teaspoons baking powder

2 tablespoons sugar

1 teaspoon salt

¼ cup milk

1 cup creamed corn

⅛ teaspoon each parsley, oregano, thyme, basil, and garlic powder

Melt the butter in a 13 x 9-inch pan. Sift together the flour, baking powder, sugar, and salt. Stir in the milk, corn, and spices. Turn the dough onto a floured surface and knead lightly. Roll to a ½-inch thickness. Cut into crescent shapes and place in the melted butter, turning so that each side is coated in butter. Cook at 450 degrees for 18 minutes. Serve warm.

Corn Woman's Magical Mush

1 cup corn meal

1 cup cold water

1 teaspoon salt

3 cups boiling water

Combine the corn meal, cold water, and salt. Pour the mixture into the boiling water. Cover and cook on low for 15 minutes, stirring when needed. This mush turns solid when cold. It may then be sliced into blocks about ½-inch thick and fried in hot oil. Serve with honey on the side, if desired. You may also dust the slices with a mixture of cinnamon and powdered sugar.

An Earth Witch's Stone Soup

Stone Soup, the popular children's tale of three soldiers who teach a village how to make soup, is a favorite among Earth Witches, who often add stones to their meal preparation because of the magical energies they impart. Simple, quick, and magical, this legendary soup is sure to please.

3 large quartz crystals, scrubbed perfectly clean and empowered to purpose

1 large pot boiling water

Salt and pepper to taste

Carrots, sliced

Cabbage, torn

5 beef bouillon cubes
1 can tomato juice
Potatoes, cubed
Celery, sliced
Bell peppers, cubed

Combine all ingredients and simmer until the vegetables are tender. You may add or subtract any vegetables you wish and season to taste. This soup also has the advantage of being high in fiber and low in calories, so it works well for dieting purposes. Remember to stir the blessings into the food by stirring in a deosil motion only. Remove the crystals before serving.

EARTH CORRESPONDENCES

Earth is considered feminine and receptive.

Season: Spring

Magical virtue: To Keep Silent

Direction: North

Time of day: Midnight

Sense: Touch

Fluid: Sweat

Power animals: Bears, bulls, lions, rabbits

Places of power: Caves, fields, bridges, meadows, gardens, mountains, crossroads, the home

Commonly associated colors: Brown, green, rust tones

Linking items: Stones, rocks, crystals, dirt, seeds, wood, pentacles, coins

EARTH STONES

Brown jasper: Brown jasper works well as an aid for grounding and centering.

Coal: Coal has a well-known reputation as a money-attracting stone, but there is more to it than that. Coal can also absorb any negative influences, making way for a clearer understand-ing of situations. It removes psychic blocks.

Emerald: Emerald has a long and distinguished magical reputa-tion. It is said to increase psychic powers, attract money and love, banish negativity, heal, improve memory, and protect the wearer. Emerald has even been assigned the power to promote your business.

Green agate: Folklore holds that washing this stone in water and then drinking the water will safeguard one against sterility. Green agate improves vision when worn. It is also reputed to reward the owner with a happy life.

Green calcite: Green calcite is known to attract prosperity.

Green jasper: Green jasper is a healing stone, both to the mind and body. It is also said to increase empathy.

Green tourmaline: Green tourmaline can be worn to increase business success and to stimulate creativity.

Jet: Jet holds the attribute of becoming electrically charged when caressed between the palms. Due to the electrical qualities of this stone, it is helpful in transformations. Jet is absorbent and can remove negative influences. It is also said to protect, in-crease psychic powers, and heal.

Malachite: Malachite holds a unique attribute: it is said to break in half to warn the owner of impending danger. It increases magical power, protects (works especially well with children), brings business success, and attracts love and peace. It is also rumored to protect against falling.

Moss agate: Moss agate is the gardener's stone. It is reputed to work as a magical safeguard to the garden. It is a healing stone and is said to be especially good for relieving a stiff neck. Moss agate can be worn to draw new friends. It works well in spells that involve happiness and riches.

Peridot: Peridot is a protective stone. It is said to be especially ef-fective in protecting the wearer against the magic and jealousy of others. Peridot is also a healing stone. It attracts prosperity, calms rages, and reduces stress.

Salt: Salt was so valuable in some parts of the world that it was used as money at one time. The religious use of salt goes back for centuries. It is cleansing and protective, increases prosperity, and works well to help one ground properly. Salt is also absorbent and therefore serves to remove any negative energies that surround a person.

Turquoise: Turquoise protects against danger. It is also said to increase courage and attract money, love, friendship, and luck. It works well as a healing stone.

EARTH HERBS

Alfalfa: Alfalfa is kept in the home to protect against hunger and poverty. It is frequently burned and the ashes scattered around the home for the same reasons. It works well in money spells as well.

Barley: Barley is a healing herb and is known specifically to relieve toothaches. It is absorbent and will remove negative influences. Barley also can be scattered for protection.

Beet: Beet juice is sometimes used as magical ink and as a substitute for blood in magical use. It is known to attract love.

Buckwheat: Buckwheat is most often used in spells concerning money and/or protection. It can be scattered, carried, or burned.

Corn: Corn works well in matters involving fertility, luck, and protection. It is frequently used in Sabbat rituals and as an offering.

Cotton: Cotton is known for its qualities of luck, healing, and protection but has other specific uses as well. Burning cotton is thought to cause rain, while scattering cotton seeds assures a productive catch when fishing and repels ghosts. Cotton cloth is excellent for magical use, as it is completely natural.

Cypress: Cypress is both a death herb and an immortality herb. It is a symbol of the crossover between the planes of life. It is a healing herb and is thought to increase one's life span.

Fern: The fern improves health and increases luck and prosperity. It is an herb of exorcism and can banish any negative influence. It is said that burning the fern's seeds will cause rain to fall, whereas carrying them will render one invisible.

Honesty: Also known as the silver dollar plant, honesty is used in prosperity spells and rituals.

Honeysuckle: Honeysuckle is healing, protective, and cleansing. It also carries the quality of increasing one's wealth and psychic powers.

Horehound: Horehound is protective and healing and is used in exorcism rituals. Drinking it is said to improve one's mental powers.

Horsetail: Horsetail is used in fertility rituals and spells.

Knotweed: Knotweed is used in bindings and health spells. It is absorbent and therefore protective.

Loosestrife: Loosestrife holds within it the attributes of peace and protection. Simply scatter it around. It can also be given to someone to cease an argument.

Mugwort: Mugwort aids in astral projection, increases strength and psychic powers, and is protective. It is very useful in any type of intuitive work. (Note: Contact with mugwort may cause dermatitis. Also, do not ingest.)

Oats: Oats are used primarily in money and prosperity spells.

Patchouli: Patchouli is useful in spells involving fertility or money. It is a good substitute for graveyard dust.

Potato: The potato is often used as a poppet for image magic. It is also protective when carried.

Primrose: The primrose is carried to attract love. When growing in the garden, it attracts fairies. It also is said to protect against madness.

Quince: Eating quinces is said to promote love. If eaten while pregnant, it is thought to increase the intelligence of the child. The quince can be carried for protection.

Rhubarb: Rhubarb pie, when fed to a lover, is said to keep that lover from straying. It is a protective amulet when worn on a string.

Rye: Rye bread served to a loved one will ensure that your love is returned.

Sagebrush: Sagebrush, also known as white sage, is a cleansing herb. It has long been used by Native Americans in smudging ceremonies to drive away any negative influences.

Tulip: The tulip serves in matters of love, prosperity, and protection. It may be carried or placed on the altar.

Turnip: Turnips in the home protect against every type of negativity. They are also used as poppets in image magic.

Vervain: The magical use of vervain has been well documented throughout the ages. It was considered the most prized of the herbs among ancient Druids. It contains the magical qualities of love, protection, purification, peace, youth, chastity, money, healing, and sleep.

Vetivert: Vetivert is most useful as a curse-breaking herb. It also attracts money and luck.

Wheat: Wheat attracts money and fertility.

Wood sorrel: Wood sorrel is a healing herb when placed in a sickroom or carried.

5

EARTH GODS AND GODDESSES

FLORA

Flora ("flourishing one") is the Roman and Greek goddess of flowers, youth, fertility, and springtime. She is also identified with the Greek goddess Chloris. It was said in the Greek myths that when Chloris (originally a nymph) was captured by Zephyrus, he gifted her with the realm of flowers in return for marrying him. So Chloris became known as the Roman Flora.

Flora was thought to give the charm to youth and the sweetness to honey and to protect the petals and give the fragrance to blossoms. She was particularly important in Roman society. Her cults are among the oldest found in Rome, and she was one of the few deities that had her own priests, who were known as the Flamen Floralis. Her bounty was the precursor of modern medicine, as Flora was not only responsible for flowers but was originally responsible for all crops. All gardens fell under her protection, and iron was strictly prohibited within them to allow the plant devas and nature spirits to prosper peacefully. Fairy folk are known for their aversion to iron.

Flora had a special garden of her own, which featured all of the mythological creatures that turned into flowers upon their deaths. Among the blossoms were Narcissus; Ajax, who became a larkspur; Clytie, who became a sunflower; Hyacinth, who had been Apollo's lover; and Adonis, who became the anemone.

Greek myths also relate a tale where Flora was responsible for the rose. While on an early morning walk through the woods, she stumbled upon the dead body of a beautiful young girl. Saddened to see such a lovely creature dead, she decided to restore her life by transforming her into the most delicate and beautiful of all flowers. In order to accomplish this, she called upon her husband, Zephyrus, god of the western wind, to blow away all of the clouds from the sky. She then called upon Apollo to send his warm rays of sunlight down as blessings. She called upon Aphrodite to add beauty and grace and Dionysus for nectar and fragrance. Everyone agreed that this was the most beautiful of all the flowers.

Flora went to work gathering dewdrops to restore life to the flower and crowned her queen of all flowers. She then called upon Aurora and Iris to spread the word about this new flower. Iris borrowed just a touch of the flower's color to spread among her rainbows, and Aurora painted the morning sky with the rose-tinted hue.

Aphrodite named the flower the rose in honor of her son Eros, the Greek god of love. Hence, roses are associated with love. Flora presented Eros with the rose as his own in the hope that it would maintain the romantic associations. Eros shared it with Harpocrates, the god of silence, as a bribe to keep secret the indiscretions of his mother, and the rose became associated with silence and secrets as well as love.

According to Roman legend, Flora also had a hand in the creation of Mars, the god of war. Juno, the wife of Jupiter, was jealous that Jupiter had given life to Minerva on his own, so she enlisted the aid of Flora to help her create a son on her own. Flora reluctantly agreed after Juno swore by the river Styx to never tell Jupiter that Flora had taken part. Flora touched Juno with a magical flower, and Mars began to grow in Juno's womb. Mars was born and went on to sire Romulus and Remus, who became the founders of Rome.

There was an ancient, and somewhat infamous, Roman festival held in Flora's honor, called the Floralia. It was celebrated annually from the end of April through the beginning of May. The dates suggest that the original purpose of the festival was to beseech Flora to refrain from allowing mildew to fall upon the crops. It is further believed that the Floralia was the inspiration for the Maypole and Mayday celebrations known today as Beltane. The Floralia featured chariot races, theater shows, games, and lavish banquets. Altars and temples were decorated with every type of flower known to humankind. The participants wore wreaths of flowers in their hair and left offerings of milk and honey.

The Floralia was also a festival known for its unrestrained pleasures. During the celebrations, marriage vows were temporarily forgotten and the celebrants allowed themselves a wide range of sexual partners. Prostitutes claimed Flora as their matron deity and celebrated her festival vigorously.

Later, as Beltane traditions evolved, Flora became known as a companion of the fairies. This eventually evolved into legends of Flora as a fairy herself. However, I believe this was borne of some confusion between the goddess Flora and the fairy Florella, who is mentioned in tomes of old as a treasure of the Earth akin to Queen Mab.

The role of the flower, and therefore that of Flora, is as important today as it was in ancient times. Almost all holidays and customs include an appropriate flower. We often send flowers to cheer those who are sick, to say farewell to those who have passed, and to celebrate mile-marker events such as birthdays, weddings, and anniversaries. We make use of the scents in perfumes and potpourris and bathing products. We make candies, jellies, wines, and salads from the petals. Flora's bounty covers everything from poisonous to healing flowers. Chamomile, jasmine, and linden flowers are commonly added to herbal teas. The purple foxglove is the base of the medicine digitalis, which is used in the treatment of heart conditions.

Flowers also have magical qualities, many of which are steeped in superstition. For instance, the daisy is often used as a divination tool in love matters by plucking the petals off while reciting, "He/she loves me, he/she loves me not." The dandelion is often used as a tool to bring one's wishes to fruition by blowing the seeds to the wind. As the wind carries the seeds, it carries one's wishes to the Goddess as well.

In the Victorian era, flowers were given their own language. A certain type of flower had a specific meaning, which was further sub-divided into categories determined by the color of the flower. For instance, to send a red rose meant "I love you," whereas to send a yellow rose meant friendship or jealousy. The number of flowers sent also had a specific meaning. It was said to be bad luck to send an even number of flowers.

When the Spanish explorer Ponce de León landed in Florida, he looked around at all the many flowers and thought he had found the land containing the Fountain of Youth. He then named the state Florida in honor of Flora.

While we may not choose to celebrate Flora the same way the Romans did, we can honor her on her special days with simple things that remind us of her presence. We can drink flower teas, add flower petals to our baths, prepare meals with edible flowers, decorate our homes and altars with garlands and wreaths, wear floral colors, or perform a ritual, or even simply take a walk through flower-strewn fields.

FAUNA

Fauna, the Roman goddess of nature and animals, was most often called Bona Dea ("the Good Goddess"), which is a title, not a name. Sometimes she was referred to as Bona Mater, which means "Good Mother." To say the actual name of Fauna was taboo in ancient Roman society. Fauna was an Earth goddess and was worshipped primarily by women. She was the daughter (sometimes represented as consort) of the nature god Faunus. It was said that after her marriage, she never laid eyes upon another man. This chastity improved her rank-ing among the gods. She was a country goddess, the protector of cattle and farmlands. She also presided over virginity and fertility in women. Today the word fauna is used to encompass all animal life.

Fauna is depicted as an old woman with pointed ears. She is represented holding the horn of plenty, and a snake is her symbol. It is said that the snake represents her phallic nature; however, men were not allowed at her temples or festivals. Her image is often found on Roman coins.

Bona Dea had two major festivals, one in May and the other on December 3 or 4. (This feast was moveable.) The festival held in December was a secret rite. It was unique because it was often held in the homes of high-ranking Roman magistrates as opposed to public temples. It was an invitation-only affair. Men were not allowed, nor was any depiction of a man welcome. Paintings and statues that included a male figure were covered up or removed. This festival was said to be a lesbian orgy; however, it has been suggested that it was actually a purification rite. It was forbidden to use the word "wine" or "myrtle," because Fauna's father had beaten her to death with a myrtle stick upon finding that she had gotten drunk. Wine was forbidden to women under Roman law. However, it was also her father who gifted her with her divinity, by repenting of her killing and bestowing divinity upon her. Wine was served at her festival but was called milk. It was traditionally kept in a jar covered with cloth. The jar was referred to as the honey pot.

Fauna's May celebration took place in her temple and was held on May 1. Wine was served in the same manner as in the December rites. The temple was decorated with vines, flowers, and plants, with the careful exclusion of myrtle. This celebration was public and open to all women. The festival was rumored to include the ritual sacrifice of a pregnant sow.

Fauna's temple was built over a cave that housed consecrated serpents. Enslaved women were prominent among the worshippers. In fact, Fauna was the only Roman deity to allow freed slaves to serve among her priestesses. Her rites were unique because she allowed high-ranking Roman women, poor women, prostitutes, and slaves to worship together side by side.

Fauna was also seen as the mother of the fairies. In this role she was a prophetess and seer. In addition, Fauna was the female essence of wildlife. In this role she was the companion of Faunus, who served as the male essence.

Fauna was a healing goddess, and her temple garden was filled with medicinal herbs. The sick were brought to her temple gardens to be healed.

DEMETER

Demeter is the Greek goddess of the grains, agriculture, and fertility. She is the daughter of the Titans Cronus and Rhea. She is an Olympian.

Demeter is so prevalent in the Greek myths that she is even responsible for the changing of the seasons. In Homer's *Hymn to Demeter*, he relates the tale. Demeter, whom Homer describes as a stately goddess, had a child with Zeus named Persephone. Unbeknown to Demeter, Zeus had planned with Hades to ensnare the young Persephone so that Hades would have a wife and therefore a queen of the Underworld. Zeus cunningly brought forth the brightly colored narcissus flower in an attempt to lure Persephone away while she was at play in the fields.

As Persephone set about gathering a bouquet of lovely irises, roses, hyacinths, violets, and crocuses, she caught sight of the most magnificent flower in the field—the narcissus. Persephone, stunned by the flower's beauty, reached out with both hands to pick it for her bouquet. As she did, the Earth opened wide, and Hades, riding upon his golden chariot led by immortal horses, snatched the beautiful Persephone and took her with him into the Underworld. Persephone cried out for her father to save her. Her cries echoed across the countryside, yet no one except Demeter heard her.

Demeter searched the Earth for nine days, grieving so desperately that she touched not a single drop of drink or bite of food. On the tenth day, at the crack of dawn, Hecate spoke with Demeter. She sent Demeter to speak with Helios, the sun god. Demeter begged Helios to tell her who had taken her beloved daughter. Helios replied that it was Zeus himself and explained the role of Hades in the plot.

Demeter was furious and grief stricken. She left Olympus and wandered to Eleusis. For a year she stilled the Earth from fruitfulness. In her grief, the flowers no longer bloomed and the gardens withered and died. The Earth was barren. Zeus sent Iris to try to persuade Demeter to come home, but Demeter would not budge. One by one, each of the gods tried to talk Demeter into returning to Olympus. She refused them all, saying that she would never return until she could lay eyes again on her beloved daughter.

Zeus, upon hearing this, sent Hermes to speak with Hades and attempt to cajole him into releasing Persephone. Hades agreed and asked only that Persephone keep him in her heart fondly. With that, he tricked her into eating three pomegranate seeds, thereby assuring that she had to return to him. Persephone happily ate the seeds and went on her way back to her mother. When Demeter was greeted by the sight of her daughter, the Earth was once again fruitful and the people rejoiced. Afraid, Demeter asked her daughter if she had eaten anything while in the Underworld, to which Persephone replied that she had eaten the seeds of a pomegranate. Demeter explained that she must live in the Underworld for one third of each year. She swore that while Persephone was on the Earth, she would hold it in bloom for her daughter's pleasure, but that while Persephone was in the Underworld, it would be barren and cold. Thus, the seasons were born.

Demeter, with her somewhat ironic sense of humor, placed the poppy in the corn and barley fields. She put all of her sweetness into the fig, which grows alongside wild herbs. As the poppy and the fig grow around the base of her more substantial foodstuffs, they represent the dark side of Demeter. The dark side is the side that holds the life and death of mortals in her hands and carries the seeds of each in her womb. Demeter represents both hunger and abundance.

In one myth, Demeter condemns a man to eternal hunger for daring to attempt to chop down her sacred grove to make a roof for his hall from the wood. The man subsequently eats until there is only one thing left to eat—himself. He devours his own limbs.

Demeter was also a goddess of fertility and, in one myth, coupled with a human in the field. The pairing produced a child. Soon after, Demeter became known as a goddess who guarded marriage and was included in ancient marriage rites. Concubines and the like were condemned to her stone gardens, where no plants could ripen and bloom. Demeter's festival, held in late autumn, was celebrated by legitimate wives and included a ritual sowing of the field. It was conducted with the hope of a harvest of beautiful children, a bounty borne from human seed.

THE DAGDA

The Dagda is the Irish father god of Earth. He is the leader of the immortal race of the Tuatha Dé Danann. The Dagda is also known as the lord of abundance. He is the god of time and magic and the protector of crops. He is the son of Danu and Beli. His name means "good god," meaning he is good at all of the things he does, not morally superior.

In Celtic mythology, it is the Dagda who is responsible for the changing of the seasons. It was said that he owned a magical harp, Daurdabla, that made the seasons change when played. He acquired this harp on a trip to the Otherworld. On the same trip he obtained the Undry, a magical cauldron said to never empty, along with the Sword of Nuada and the Lia Fáil, which is also known as the Stone of Life. These three items, along with the Spear Luin, are thought to represent the four elements.

The Dagda is represented in a somewhat comical form. He is most often depicted as a large man with a paunch belly wearing a too-short tunic that leaves his genitals bare and exposed, hauling around his magical mallet in a cart. The mallet was said to kill nine men in a single blow and restore them to life with the handle. Although he was frequently the subject of jokes, the Dagda was held in the highest esteem. The Celts believed that even the highest being possessed a flaw or two.

While he was the main consort of the Morrigan, the Dagda was known to have many other lovers. It was said that he was one of lusty appetites, and when he came upon the raven-haired Morrigan washing clothes in a stream, he walked up behind her and began having his way with her. The Morrigan found the interlude so satisfactory that she backed him in battle the next day.

In one tale, the Dagda was sent by Lugh to spy on the Fomorians. He went to their camp and asked for a truce, which was granted. The Fomorians decided to mock the Dagda by making a porridge. The Dagda's weakness for porridge was well-known. The Fomorians made a huge amount and proclaimed that unless the Dagda ate every bite, he would be killed. He ate every bite and promptly fell asleep. When he awoke, he found the Fomorians laughing at him. The Dagda forced himself to leave, which was no easy feat considering his bloated, swollen belly. On his way, he chanced upon a girl who threw him into the mud and demanded she be returned to her father's house. The Dagda asked who her father was, and she replied that he was the king of the Fomorians. The Dagda and the girl wrestled about and ended up making love. As she was smitten at this point, she helped the Dagda defeat the Fomorians in battle by singing spells against them.

The Dagda's main consort was Boann, and they are the parents of the Celtic goddess Brigid. He is also the father of the fairy king Midir and many others.

The Dagda is said to rule today from the Otherworld, as his life on this plane was ended in battle by a woman named Cethlion. Once defeated, he led the Tuatha Dé Danann through a fairy mound to live underground in the Otherworld.

CORN WOMAN

In Native American lore, it is the Corn Woman who is known as the "first mother." It is said that there was once a time of great famine. The Corn Woman went to her husband and asked that he kill her. The husband, distraught, went to the tribe's teacher, who confirmed that he must do as his wife asked. With great reluctance, he complied. He dragged her body around a field and buried her in the center of it. In a few months, corn and tobacco filled the field, saving the tribe from starvation.

In the Pawnee tribe, Corn Woman held rule over the west, while Buffalo Woman held the east. Together they guaranteed that the tribe had both meat and corn.

In one of the earliest tales, we find that the Corn Woman emerged from an older world, one in which animals were not slaughtered for food and hides but rather were treated as kin. The old world had a greater respect for life, be it animal or human. The people began to lose balance, and greed crept in. The deer set forth a punishment for any who would eat of its flesh—man's first known disease. Corn Woman thought it was time to begin again and restore balance and harmony to the people.

She watched her grandsons preparing to go out to hunt and asked them to stay. She said she would cook the finest meal they had ever tasted. The grandsons replied that they were hunters and must hunt. Corn Woman nodded sadly and went about creating her meal, but not before she asked her grandsons to respect the animal life they came across in the forest. The grandsons laughed.

Corn Woman cooked, all the while singing and blessing the food. When her grandsons returned home, she saw that they had killed a wild pig. She said nothing. They sat down and began to eat of her feast. Loudly, the grandsons proclaimed the food the best they had ever tasted and proceeded to eat their fill. They asked her where she had gotten the corn, but she did not answer. She just listened to the compliments and smiled.

The next day, the young men again reached for their weapons. Corn Woman cooked again. The aromas from her kitchen reached them out in the woods as they hunted. That day, they brought home a slain deer. Corn Woman said nothing. The grandsons gifted her with the deer, and she recognized it as an honor and so returned it to the forest. She sang long into the night, invading the dreams of her grandsons.

When they awoke the next morning, instead of reaching for their weapons, the grandsons asked Corn Woman to make them breakfast. She did, and they ate until they were sleepy again. When they awoke from their naps, they gathered their weapons and set about preparing to hunt. Corn Woman asked them not to go. She said, "We have so much food already." The grandsons said they were hunters and set out toward the forest. Corn Woman called after them to respect animal life.

While on their hunt, one of the young men asked the other where Corn Woman got all the corn she was using to cook with. The other man replied that he did not care and that he knew Corn Woman would only give him what was good for him. They returned home with a turkey but once again sat down to a delightful meal of corn.

After many days of wondering, the younger of the two grandsons decided to sneak back to the home and find out where Corn Woman was getting all of the corn. As he watched, she slapped her sides and the corn fell out of her body and into a basket at her side. He ran to tell his older brother. The eldest grandson was upset. He said, "This is a bad thing, an unnatural thing. We cannot eat our grandmother. Something has taken hold of her."

That night, the grandsons returned home in fear. Corn Woman piled their plates high, but the two could not eat. Her heart grew heavy as she realized that they knew her secret. She began to age rapidly before their eyes. The youngest started to cry and beg forgiveness. Corn Woman replied, "Listen well, child. For I have not long as I am to tell you all you need know. I am the Corn Mother. I am here for your abundance, harmony, health, and peace. When I pass, you are to drag my body through the field and plant me in the center. I will come back to you as a tall, glorious plant, with yellow hair at my fruit. Do not eat all of the seeds; save some for the planting again the next year, so that I might be with you forever." The grandsons swore to do as she wished. Thereafter they refused to hunt unless they were on the verge of starvation. Hence, balance and harmony returned to the people.

In the Navajo tribe, we find variations of the Corn Woman. According to Navajo beliefs, there was a Corn Girl (yellow corn) and a Corn Boy (white corn) sent forth by the creator god to bring corn to the tribe. Corn was sacred and the main food of the people and was also used in religious ceremonies. Shamans' masks were fed corn meal to "bring them into being," or animate them.

The Aztecs have their own version of the Corn Woman in Chicomecoatl, the goddess of sustenance. It was thought that yearly sacrifices held in her honor assured a good crop. Each year a young girl was chosen to represent Chicomecoatl and was ritually decapitated. Her blood was poured over a statue of the goddess as an offering. She was skinned and her flesh was then worn by a priest.

The Hopi and Pueblo tribes have the Blue Corn Maiden as their representative of Corn Woman. On a cold winter day, the Blue Corn Maiden went out in search of firewood. Normally this was not a task for her. While she was out searching, she ran across Winter Katsina, the spirit of winter. When Winter Katsina saw the Blue Corn Maiden, he immediately fell in love. He took her back to his house, whereupon he blocked the door and windows with ice and snow. He was very kind to her, but she was sad. She wanted to go home and make the blue corn grow for her people.

While Winter Katsina was out one day going about his duties, Blue Corn Maiden sneaked out and found four blades of Yucca plant. She started a fire. As she did, in walked Summer Katsina, carrying more yucca and blue corn. When Winter Katsina returned, the two fought. Seemingly getting nowhere, they sat down to talk. They agreed that Blue Corn Maiden would live half the year with her people, during the reign of Summer Katsina, and the people would have corn. During the other half of the year, she would live with Winter Katsina, and the people would have no corn.

THE GREEN MAN

The Green Man is the vision of a face in the leaves—a face surrounded by or made from leaves. He embodies nature—wild, free, and primitive. He is known as Cernunnos, Herne, Pan, Faunus, Puck, John Barleycorn, and the Horned God, to name just a few. The Green Man is the male essence of nature. His face graces more churches and cathedrals than one can imagine, a unique feat for a pagan god.

Cernunnos is the Celtic god of nature. He is commonly seen as a horned god. The horn is a symbol of virility and fertility. As Cernunnos, his worship can be traced back to the Iron Age Celts through historical artifacts; however, very little is known about how he was regarded or worshipped.

In Britain, the nature god is known as Herne the Hunter. Herne was a favorite of King Richard II. He saved the king from a raging stag and was severely wounded. A stranger tied the antlers of the stag to Herne's head, claiming his hunting talent as payment. Herne, devastated at this loss of talent, ran off into the woods. Later, a man found his corpse hanging on a tree. Herne is said to appear in spectral form and to indulge in his favorite pastime—hunting. He is said to lead the Wild Hunt.

Pan is the Greek nature god who watches over the shepherds and their flocks. He is known as Faunus in Roman mythology. Pan is considered to be older than the Olympians. He gave Apollo the secrets of prophecy and gifted Artemis with her hunting dogs.

Pan was originally an Arcadian god. He is described as a man with the legs, horns, and hindquarters of a goat. Due to the Olympians disdain of Arcadians, they always treated Pan as a second-class god. However, his popularity among the primitive mountain people of Arcadia never lessened.

Pan was thought to inspire a type of sudden fear. In fact, the word panic is a derivation of his name. Pan was a lecherous god and was well-known for his indulgence in amorous affairs. One nymph named Pitys turned into a pine tree to escape his advances, while another, Syrinx, turned into river reeds. At the exact moment that Syrinx did so, the wind blew, creating a melodic sound. Pan, much intrigued, picked several of the reeds and turned them into his signature pan pipes.

All of the deities that are considered to be the male essence of nature are thought to follow a cycle of life, death, and rebirth in sync with the seasons.

PART TWO
WATER

6

THE PATH OF THE WATER WITCH

Water Witches are sometimes called Sea Witches, but many of them find a calling with inland creeks, rivers, and lakes. It is rare for them to limit themselves to any one type of body of water. They generally align with all forms, including rain.

In most mythologies, humans sprang from the Earth, but the gods themselves came from water. Egyptian theory states that the sun god Re was born from the primordial waters. Today, scientists can back that theory. NASA scientists theorize that water exists in heavy quantities in the universe. It works as a coolant. The water vapors in outer space allow for the condensing of clouds. Once a cloud condenses enough, it becomes a star.

Water reflects; the Water Witch does the same. If you yell at her, she will yell back at you. If you are kind to her and treat her well, she will be kind and treat you well in return. She is very fair. She shares many qualities with her sister Earth Witch, as the Earth is 90 percent water. Among those qualities is the core belief of taking complete responsibility for her actions. The Water Witch accepts that every move she makes can cause ripples across the surface of the water, and moves accordingly.

Water is considered a feminine force, and the Water Witch may prefer an alliance with the Goddess, all the while recognizing and maintaining that the God is within the Goddess. She can sometimes relate closely to Dianic Witches in this preference.

The Water Witch can see things that those on other paths cannot. In fact, the human sense of sight belongs in her realm. Just as the seas teem with life that we have yet to discover and understand, the Water Witch knows that there is much more to our world than what is within our eyesight. While she can be highly superstitious, for the most part she simply knows that there is more just waiting to be discovered, as well as some things that humanity has known about and forgotten over the ages. The old phrase "out of the blue" speaks volumes about the ability of the Water Witch to tune in to her intuition. She is often very gifted in divination practices. Tarot is usually her divinatory tool of choice, but she also has a talent for dowsing.

The Water Witch sees little that she considers an obstacle. She understands that her fate is in her hands, and if she cannot flow through something, she will flow around it. Once her mind is made up, very little can stop her from obtaining what she wants. Because water exists in three forms on Earth, the Water Witch can be considered a formidable force. She will not admit to any weaknesses.

The Water Witch has a close link to the feminine side of nature. She understands reproduction and is akin to her sister Earth Witch in this manner as well. Menstruation falls in the realm of the Water Witch. Because of this, she is instrumental in moon-lodge practices and coming-of-age rites. Her sister Earth Witch may focus more on the rebirth cycle, while the Water Witch is more in touch with creation.

The Water Witch specializes in healing, cleansing, beauty, emotions, intuition, and energy. Her magical style is usually based on instinct. If the feeling hits her to perform a cleansing, she will. She does not necessarily worry about correspondences and timing. Her timing is completely her own—she will not be rushed by others into decisions or action. Schooled in water magic, ice magic, and snow magic, the

Water Witch can tell you all about the role of water in the metaphysical and physical realms.

Winter is the season when the Water Witch's power is at its peak. She holds within herself the ability to transform fluidity to solid form during the winter, the same way that water turns to ice. It is during this season that the Water Witch should turn her view inward and evaluate her goals. She often redefines herself through the process. Because of this, a Water Witch grows stronger every year. She understands that just as dry ice is sticky, it is her role to hold things together.

Throughout the winter months, the Water Witch is abnormally busy, even for her active lifestyle. Because she is at her highest power and incarnated in all three of her forms during these months, she may be short of temper. When you add to that the fact that artificial heat (fire, an evaporating influence on water) is usually pumped into the home during this time, and families tend to be cooped up in the same space, you may have one cranky, stressed-out Water Witch on your hands. She longs for room to spread out and flow. A simple snowfall can ease her mind and soothe her spirit; she draws strength from it. If that is not an option, a long bath or a cup of hot tea usually helps. Rest assured that if you visit her in the winter months, she will be a very gracious hostess, regardless of the timing. The Water Witch is known for her generous hospitality.

Her home décor is usually unthemed, with whimsy being the main rule. The Water Witch may have a quirky collection of glass objects, prisms (she tends to like sparkly things), tons of throw pillows, and an aquarium. Cool blues and greens are often primary colors in both her wardrobe and her home.

Due to her busy lifestyle, the Water Witch frequently has to let the housework slide somewhat. Although she prefers all things to be clean, she also understands that there must be "salt in the sea." In other words, a small amount of dirt is inevitable, and she is able to live with that comfortably. She absolutely cannot stand clutter, though. It drives her to distraction.

Another common trait of the Water Witch is a quirky sense of humor. It simply cannot be defined. Some of the things she says seem to come from outer space in their relation to the topic, yet they can make you laugh as nothing else will. This is intentional—the Water Witch is lighthearted. But just when you begin to think she has never had a deep thought in her life, she will prove you wrong. When it comes to serious conversation, the Water Witch can often put her finger on an aspect of the situation that the other Elemental Witches do not see. The Water Witch is very wise.

Like her mythical brethren the mermaids and water nymphs, the Water Witch tends to love long hair. She may keep it pulled back in a ponytail due to a lack of time, but she lets it grow nonetheless. The effects that water has on the body are directly in line with the metaphysical attributes of the Water Witch. Usually beautiful, she is often younger looking in appearance than in age and has a long memory and attention span and bright, shining eyes.

Because the Water Witch always considers every side of an argument before making up her mind, she may be slow to assume a position. Rest assured that when a Water Witch states her opinion, it has been well thought out. She is open-minded and fair. Her strength lies in her dual nature and ability to see the points of view of others. And like water, she will find her way into all of the small nooks and crannies of a situation. She may initially choose an answer based on instinct, but if new facts come to light, she will often change her mind. She is flexible.

Those on the water path often find a calling in helping others. They make wonderful therapists, psychiatrists, obstetricians, pediatricians, or service personnel. Often, people are attracted to their soothing nature and come to them for advice. Like a waterbed, a reflecting pool, or a relaxing bath, Water Witches project an aura of serenity and comfort.

The Water Witch may be seen as moody, but like the sea herself, she is often in motion. She rarely slows down. She is full of energy and always on the go. And like the sea, her moods swing with the tides. The moon holds sway over the tides, and one can easily draw a parallel between the moon and the Water Witch's emotional patterns.

THE DARK SIDE OF THE WATER WITCH

Water rules the emotions, and the Water Witch has a predisposition to think with the heart and not the head. As she is devoted to water, she believes wholeheartedly that a tiger can change its stripes by virtue of cleansing away the negative. She will give a second chance in the case of an innocent mistake. However, if crossed intentionally, the Water Witch will hold a grudge until the end of time. She is a wall builder and will not hesitate to block out anyone who deserves it. Her code of justice is so strict that she often entertains notions of revenge. She is known to overdo it in these matters.

In personal matters, the Water Witch's intuition does not function at its fullest capacity. She can be quick to assume a slight was intended by an innocent remark and operate strictly on that notion, regardless of its truthfulness. Unfortunately, once this happens, the Water Witch can muddy her own waters.

WATER WITCH LORE

Rains

One of the most obscure and most exciting natural phenomena is colored rain. During the evaporation process, the rain sometimes picks up colored pigments in the dust or dirt near an area or in the atmosphere. The result is rain that leaves a colored stain on the ground or on exposed objects. There have been reports of green, yellow, black, red, and brown rain in various places all over the world.

In 2001, almost the entire country of India was visited by colored rain. Scientists theorized that it was due to a meteorite stirring up dust in the atmosphere. A few years earlier, Afghanistan was visited by yellow rain, which was thought to be caused by a heavy concentration of pollen in the air.

The red rains have been referred to as "rains of blood" by many and can be quite alarming if one does not know what they are. The red minerals picked up over clay-laden lands can cause this rain to be bright scarlet, exactly like blood. Cases have been investigated for hundreds of years in the southeastern states of the United States. The most amazing part of the blood-rain cases is that many eyewitnesses claimed that actual tissue matter fell along with the rain. Scientists say this is an exaggeration due to a hysterical reaction to red rain, but other reports speculate that it may possibly have been bird tissue.

The red rains are thought to be more dangerous than the other colors of rain. It has been said that the red rain burned those it fell upon. As red is also the color of anger, this is not at all surprising. But what is surprising is the sudden appearance of swarms of butterflies directly after a red rain.

In parts of the world that boast of extremely high mountains, red and pink snow has been known to fall. This is commonly called "watermelon snow" and has been said to even smell like watermelon. Aristotle mentioned this type of colored snow in some of his work. Other colors of snow include green, yellow, and orange, although they are not as common as watermelon snow.

Merfolk

Whole books have been written about mermaids and mermen. The mermaids are the female version of this race of water beings. They are said to be exceptionally beautiful and have the upper body of a human woman and the lower body of a large fish. Scottish folklore states that human legs are just beneath the fish scales.

Merfolk are usually spotted by fisherman, most often while the merfolk are sunning themselves on rocks. They are said to have enchanting singing voices and have been credited with leading many sailors to their deaths. They are also said to be portents of particularly violent storms.

As members of the fairy realm, merfolk are thought to be soulless. It is a common belief that they can gain a soul by marrying a human and remaining on dry land. Moreover, it is also commonly accepted that to gain a mermaid wife, a human must steal her comb, cap, or mirror and then hide it. If the mermaid cannot find it, she will remain on land. Eventually, she will be overcome with homesickness and slip quietly back into the water.

Mermen, in stark contrast to the beautiful females of the species, are said to be ugly. They have green hair, large mouths, snub noses, and green teeth. They reportedly give off a "wild" vibration. They are said to be adversarial and cause storms or large waves unless offerings are made to them. Frequently, the ship's captain would tend to this by placing any dead bodies with the offerings and then tossing them overboard.

One well-documented merfolk encounter took place in Denmark, in the year 1723. It seems that a royal commission had become so plagued with merfolk tales that they set out to disprove their existence. Along the way, they themselves encountered a merman. He was said to have risen from the water and stared at them. After a few minutes of this, they were so disturbed that they turned the ship around. Once they did, the merman growled at them and dove back into the water.

There are hundreds of accounts from people claiming to have seen a mermaid. Even Christopher Columbus claimed to have encountered mermaids in his voyage to the West Indies.

Some tales of merfolk-type creatures are quite ancient. The Babylonian god Oannes, who was human from the waist up and a fish from the waist down, was popular around the year 300 BC. Oannes was credited with imparting knowledge and culture to humans. Other deities of the merfolk type were worshipped in India, Greece, and Rome.

In ancient China, around 3322 BC, the deities of Fuxi and his wife, Nu Gua, were thought of as the founders of Chinese civilization after the great flood. Half human, half fish, they created the system of the I Ching.

Wishing Wells, Miracle Springs, and Legendary Fountains

Each well is said to have its own guardian spirit. The guardian spirits of wells are sometimes deities and other times nymphs or sprites. Water drawn at dawn from a particularly deep well is said to cure a toothache. Traditionally, a well should be fed a slice of bread each year on New Year's Day.

In some parts of the world, it is also traditional to dress the well with flowers. This tradition goes back to the ancient Romans and the festival of Fontinalia. It is an honor bestowed upon the guardian of that particular well, as a thank-you and a remembrance. Fontinalia was celebrated by the Romans annually on October 13, in honor of Fontus, the Roman god of fountains, springs, and wells.

Wishing wells specifically collect offerings from those petitioning the guardian spirit of the well. The petitioner must ask for the wish to be granted silently or by whispering. Typical offerings are coins, pebbles, and pins. This custom derives from an older custom that utilized stones. It is thought that when you toss your coin into the well, the guardian spirit will then decide whether or not to bless you with what you desire.

One rare example of the power of a well is St. Elian's Well in Wales. This well is said to have the power to place a curse instead of granting a wish. In order to petition it to do so, you must write your wish on paper and lower it into the well in a lead casket.

In Norse mythology, the gods themselves held meetings at Urd's Well (the Well of Wyrd). It was this well that kept the Yggdrasil tree (the World Tree) healthy and thriving.

A curious legend about Demeter's sacred well relates that people who were sick could divine their future with it. They would lower a mirror on a cord to the water's surface. They would pray and perform a ritual (which sometimes included a sacrifice). After the ritual, they would use the mirror as a scrying tool and discern from their own intuition what the oncoming days held for them. This well was reputed to be extremely accurate.

Rituals were often performed at wells, springs, or fountains. These were the most common places for shrines and altars to be erected. Ishtar, the Babylonian moon goddess, is closely associated with springs. Many of her temples were placed in areas that contained a natural spring.

The modern country of Greece boasts of well over seven hundred natural hot mineral springs. All of them are touted to have a healing effect on the body and regenerative properties, due to the presence of natural minerals.

The natural thermal springs at Skala Thermi, on the Greek island of Lesvos, are sacred to Artemis and are recommended for people with asthma, any female problems, kidney and bladder troubles, high blood pressure, or liver ailments.

Many natural springs are connected to dreams. They tend to have a radioactive quality and cause the visitor to become drowsy. Sleeping at such sites is thought to induce prophetic dreams.

Ponce de León, the famous Spanish explorer, spent his life devoted to the quest to find the legendary Fountain of Youth. When he stumbled upon a natural spring in what is now the city of Saint Augustine, Florida, he thought he had found it. The Fountain of Youth was reputed to have magical waters that guaranteed the drinker a restoration of youth.

The Fountain of Kanathos was said to have a special magical power. It was thought to have restored the goddess Hera's virginity on her annual bathing sojourns.

The fountain Elivagar was in the center of Niflheim (the Norse version of the Underworld). Unlike the clean, clear water of most fountains, Elivagar produced a black, poisonous sludge. It fed the eleven rivers of Niflheim.

In China, the fountain at Pon Lai was believed to gift the drinker with one thousand lives. This legend dates back to the Chin Dynasty, circa 265–420 CE.

Bathing in and drinking the miracle waters was a favorite pastime and healing influence in many cultures. The Roman bathhouses emerged as an alternative within city walls to the natural springs in Greece. Known for their sumptuous appointments, the larger Roman baths usually had separate areas for men and women. The smaller ones would permit women only at certain times and men only at other times. In the bathing chambers, one would find hot pools, cool pools, saunas, and steam rooms as well as gardens, reading rooms, and libraries. They were social places, where people gathered to enjoy the relaxing effects of the waters and the company of others. Often the Romans would have oil rubbed into their skin before partaking in the baths. Then they would steam and take a hot bath followed by a cold bath, and lastly they would oil themselves again.

The Native Americans, ancient Japanese, and Scandinavians made use of steam baths as a purifying rite. Known as saunas today, these ancient sweatbox rites were thought of as purely spiritual acts, separate from hygienic bathing practices.

The thought that water could cleanse the spirit has prevailed throughout the ages. The "baptismal" attributes of water were utilized in most cultures. The ancient Japanese had the custom of "the first bath" for newborn children. Water also played a role in the Eleusinian Mysteries. It is believed that the participants would bathe in the ocean, and when they emerged, they were given a new name to match their renewed spirit.

The Native Americans were the first culture of people to understand the duality of water. They associated each water site individually with positive or negative vibrations. Certain places were thought to be bad, and they would not drink from them. They tried to always show proper respect to the water spirits. In fact, they were slightly afraid of them. For example, if a hunter was boastful or prideful over his kill and did not show the proper respect and thanksgiving to the water spirit, he could be shot with an invisible arrow that was believed to cause illness. Many of them believed that drinking from a spring at night would also cause them to be shot with an illness arrow.

In other parts of the world, we find legends of horrifying creatures such as Jenny Greenteeth, a water fairy in northern England who every seven years would claim the life of a human by dragging the person to the bottom of the water and waiting for him or her to drown.

Legendary Rivers

Rivers in general have some rather dark folklore about them. In Scotland and Ireland, superstition holds that each river demands one life as its due each year. Rivers are a common theme in mythology as gateways to the other side, the land of death. The river Styx, for example, was the portal to the land of the Underworld.

Styx was considered so holy that to swear by it was sacred, even for the gods. The person making the promise was bound by the river to tell the truth. The water was undrinkable—it would cause even a deity to lose their voice for nine years. If one swore an oath by the Styx and did not keep it, Zeus himself would force the oath breaker to drink from its waters.

In order to cross the river Styx into the land of Hades, one had to pay the ferryman, Charon. The ancient Greeks buried the dead with coins under their tongues to ensure that their loved ones would be carried safely across.

Styx, which translates to "river of hate," was only one river in the Greek Underworld. The other four rivers in the Underworld were as follows:

Acheron: The "river of woe"

Cocytus: The "river of lamentation"

Phlegethon: The "river of fire"

Lethe: The "river of forgetfulness"

In Norse folklore, the Underworld was known as Niflheim. It was ruled over by the goddess Hel. It was said to have eleven icy cold rivers, which eventually emptied into the river Styx. The river Slith was a combination of floating blades, blood, tears, waste, and poison. The river Gjall was called the "river of echoes." It had many waterfalls, strong currents, and bones floating in its waters.

Though the connection between rivers and the Underworld in folklore may be a dark theme, rivers have their light side too. It is said that no vampire, demon, ghost, or attacking spirit can follow one across a river.

Rivers with an inspirational overtone far outnumber the darker rivers of myth. The Nile, the Ganga, and the Niger, just to name a few, are thought to be life-giving. Millions of lives depend on the waters from these rivers. The Nile River is said to be responsible for Egypt's existence, as it could never be what it is without her power. The people also credit the river with growth in the areas of friendly personalities, generosity, and love. When it comes to rivers in general, the Water Witch understands that sitting on a riverbank and watching the sun sparkle on the water is actually a way of soaking up the love of the universe.

Water Horses

Here is yet another dark little tidbit about water. In Celtic regions, there was a creature called a water horse. This creature was so powerful-looking and enchanting that once seen, a person could not help but wish to ride on its back. If he tried, he would soon regret it. It would run so fast that a human would not be able to catch his breath, whereupon the horse would plunge back under the water, carrying the rider with it to a watery grave.

Thought to be most prevalent in the month of November, these magnificent creatures could shapeshift into human form. In this capacity they were known to eat their victims. It was said that the only way to kill a water horse was to hold it over a roaring fire until it melted.

In Scotland, this creature was known as the water bull and was a guardian of the entries into the fairy realm.

The Lady of the Lake

In the Camelot legends, the Lady of the Lake is a mysterious personage. Foster mother to Lancelot, it was said that she raised him beneath the water, grooming him to become the powerful knight he became. She also gifted Arthur with the magical sword of Excalibur at the behest of Merlin, and later took it back when it was thrown into the lake. She was one of the three ladies who lead Arthur to Avalon after his death.

Because she is identified as many different women in various texts, it is argued that "Lady of the Lake" may have been a title instead of a name, used to identify a high priestess. It is further suggested that the lady was a water goddess or a creature from the fairy realm.

Judging by her actions, we can perceive that the Lady of the Lake's essence was wise and benevolent and tended to function according to intuition.

Atlantis

According to Plato, the island of Atlantis vanished beneath the ocean around 9000 BC. It was a very rich land, created by Poseidon. The story goes that Poseidon fell in love with a mortal woman, Cleito. He created the island for her and surrounded it with walls. She bore him five sets of twin sons, who ruled the people inhabiting the island.

Due to their wealth and political power, the people of Atlantis became corrupt and greedy. Zeus was outraged. He gathered the gods together and they decided upon a fitting punishment. Soon after, Atlantis disappeared beneath the water.

Atlantis was said to have a unique metal, which has never been found elsewhere on Earth. This metal was called orichalc and was second only to gold in value.

The roads and walls of Atlantis are believed to have been discovered near the tropical island of Bimini (located about fifty miles east of Miami, Florida), the same island that the natives described to Ponce De León as the actual home of the Fountain of Youth. However, whether or not these are the actual walls—indeed, whether or not Atlantis even existed—is highly debated. Clairvoyant Edgar Cayce claimed that it did.

Theories abound on where Atlantis might have been and how it was destroyed. Some claim it was during the great flood, while others say it was due to a volcanic eruption. Still others say it was covered with water when the Ice Age ended. Like the recent discovery of the planet Vulcan (which was named Sedna), perhaps scientists will one day be able to prove the existence of Atlantis.

WATER MAGIC

The properties of water are both constant and variable at the same time. Water exists on the Earth in three forms: solid (ice), liquid, and gas (evaporated). Water magic is very versatile; it incorporates techniques that bring about changes both within and without. For water magic to occur within, one must consume the water or call upon that aspect of the self. For it to occur without, one must bathe in it, swim in it, cleanse with it, etc.

Not all liquid magic belongs in the realm of water. For instance, brews that incorporate vinegar or alcohol as the primary ingredient fall in the domain of fire.

The magical properties of particular types of water can be used for the following purposes:

Creeks and streams: Purification, harmony, cleansing.

Dew: General health, eyesight, beauty. Dew is said to be especially powerful if gathered at dawn on Beltane.

Fog and mists: Creativity, balance, partnerships.

Ice: Transformations, balance, creativity.

Pond or lake water: Peace, contentment, relaxation, self-reflection.

Rain water: Energy, protection, cleansing. The first rain that falls in the month of May is considered sacred to the Water Witch.

River water: Cleansing, moving forward, protection.

Seawater: Health, magical power, manifestation of goals. An old Welsh belief states that a spoonful of seawater a day will ensure a long and healthy life.

Snow: Transformations, balance.

Spring water: Growth, holy water, cleansing, protection, prosperity.

Swamp and waste water: Banishing, binding.

Waterfalls: Power, energy, success.

Well water: Healing, wishes, intuition.

The Water Witch also has an attachment to the areas surrounding the water, which can be used for the following magical purposes:

Beaches: Rituals, spells, fascinations, meditations.

Harbors: To promote abundance and prosperity; to serve as an aid in banishing things.

Riverbanks: To increase personal power.

In Santería practices, water from particular environments is offered as food to specific Orishas, as follows:

Ogun and Babalu-Aye: Pond water

Oya: Rain water

Oshun: River water

Yemaya: Seawater

In addition, Santería incorporates the use of a special cleansing water called omiero. Omiero is comprised of sacred herbs, belonging to the Orisha being petitioned, and water. It is steeped upon coals to bring out the magical properties. The making of omiero is complicated and has a full ceremony attached to it. The resulting product is used for initiation purposes.

HOLY WATERS

The Water Witch puts great store in the powers of her holy waters. Natural waters on which she performs a blessing are usually the best for use as holy water, as they are pure. Clear quartz is often added to boost the power of the water even more. A blessing from a Water Witch removes all negative vibrations and recycles them within the water. In effect, she is using the power of water to cleanse the water. The Water Witch knows that all water is blessed from the start by the Goddess. All that is required of a Witch to bless water is a simple statement of intent, something along the lines of, "I cast out all negativity and proclaim this water as pure and good. Blessed am I to have access to it, and blessed is it, for it is my mother's tears and love." She might choose to be more eloquent at times, but usually she goes with the flow and follows her instincts.

Water collection methods can be elaborate or simple. A jar placed outside during a thunderstorm, a special gourd dipper used to pull water from a crystal-clear brook, or simply cupping your hands under a natural spring—all of these methods are proper.

THE IMPORTANCE OF SEA SALT

In maritime lore, seawater was thought to cleanse a person thoroughly, absorbing any bad luck, due to the salt content of the water. Throwing salt into a fire for nine consecutive days was thought to break any chain of bad luck, while throwing salt at a person was sure to bring her grief.

SHELL MAGIC

Shells hold universal energies. They can be used for spell work in the same manner as crystals or herbs:

Abalone: The abalone shell is often featured on the Water Witch's altar as a focal point. It can be used to hold smaller items, to burn things, or simply to add extra power to a spell.

Clam: Clam shells are used for purification and love spells. They can be placed in charm bags.

Conch: Conch shells work best in love spells.

Coral: Coral works well in matters of health and healing.

Cowries: Sacred to the Orisha Oya, the cowrie shell has a prestigious magical pedigree. Due to its vulva-like appearance, this shell is frequently used upon altars as a representation of the Goddess. Cowries work well in matters involving money and prosperity.

Oysters: Oyster shells work best in matters pertaining to luck. They are said to promote good fortune. They make wonderful additions to charm bags.

POTIONS, BREWS, AND ELIXIRS

Potions, brews, and elixirs are all essentially the same thing, with a few small differences. Potions are made from liquid ingredients or worked into a liquid base. Elixirs usually have crystals added to the liquid for extra power. Brews usually require some sort of heating process. (Soup and tea are both brews.)

Peaceful Night's Rest Brew

5 tablespoons lavender flowers
A saucepan of clear water

Bring the mixture to a boil, then reduce heat and boil gently for two minutes. Strain the lavender buds from the water. Add the scented water to your laundry when you wash your bed linens.

Energy Boost Elixir

1 clear quartz crystal
3 ounces orange juice

1 tablespoon honey
1 teaspoon lemon juice

Charge the crystal with intent. Clearly state that the crystal will absorb positive energy, which it will impart to you at a later time. Mix all the ingredients together. Say, "I call the universal energy of white light and love to impart energy into this drink." Drink it quickly, but do not allow the crystal to flow into your mouth, to avoid choking. Say, "So it is done!"

Kiss Me Potion

½ teaspoon vanilla extract
½ teaspoon honey
1 teaspoon instant coffee

Mix all the ingredients together while charging with intent. State aloud that this potion will draw romantic, loving, and sexual energies of a positive and desirable nature to you. You may want to gently heat the extract and honey first, so the coffee crystals fully dissolve. Dab this potion on your lips and pulse points every few hours, to attract romance. This potion is very versatile and flexible. Mix a spoonful into a warm beverage and serve to the one you want to kiss you.

FLOOR WASHES

A floor wash is made by adding specific herbs, oils, crystals, and other ingredients to water and then using the solution to wash a surface. The reasoning behind this practice is to infuse the surface with the vibrations of the wash, so that it will then attract or dispel the corresponding energies. For example, if you were owed payment for services and the check was late, you might want to wash your mailbox with a money-drawing wash.

Traditional methods call for you to scrub the floor on your hands and knees. The repetitive motion and low concentration level needed allow for a shift in consciousness to take place. Incorporating a chant as you wash will boost the powers of the wash and help your goal to manifest even faster. Remember to be as specific as possible in the wording of your chant.

Fast Money Wash

1 teaspoon cinnamon

5 cloves

1 tablespoon orange zest

1 teaspoon ginger

1 teaspoon nutmeg

3 drops pine essential oil

Combine all ingredients, empowering them one by one by stating aloud the specific function each will perform. For example, if you were to use rosemary as an ingredient in a memory potion, you would need to say, "the rosemary will serve as a memory enhancer," or something of that nature. Then bless the ingredients on your altar. Let the mixture rest in a dark area for a week. Take it out once a day, shake it, bless it, and then return it. If possible, charge this potion under a full moon during its week of rest, to magnify the magical properties it contains. (The power of a full moon is present for three days before and three days after the actual night of the full moon.) After a week, add the mixture to a bucket of warm, clear water for washing. *Important note:* This wash seems to have the side effect of making those that come into contact with it hungry. It smells wonderful.

Wishy Washy

This magical wash is thought to bring about your wishes.

1 tablespoon sage

1 tablespoon vanilla

1 tablespoon sandalwood

Combine all the ingredients in a pan, empowering them one by one. Bring to a boil, and boil for 3 minutes. Add the mixture to cold wash water, and bless it. Say, "My wishes will come to me, to take care of myself and my family. With harm to none and good will to all, mother mine, hear my call. Bring these desired goals to me, so that me and mine will blessed be."

MAGICAL BATHS

Most Witches partake in magical bathing. A magical bath is considered important for cleansing the spirit, the same way regular bathing is for cleansing the body. Magical baths work best by candlelight, with herbal, oil, and/or salt additions, corresponding to the need. You can also use magical bathing to allow the water to work on you and impart some of its wisdom to you, through your immersion in it. In this manner, a magical bath can be used for spell casting.

Friendship Drawing Bath

    1 square piece of linen, about 2 x 2 inches
    Piece of string
    Handful of Epsom salts
    Pinch of cinnamon
    3 rose petals (yellow, if you can find them)
    Pinch of orange zest
    Pinch of lemon balm
    Pinch of red carnation petals
    Pinch of sage
    3 drops honey
    1 moonstone or rose quartz

Tie all of the herbal ingredients into the square of linen. Whisper to the sachet your intent to attract new friends. Crush the herbs in the sachet a bit with your hands. Place the sachet in the bathtub, under the faucet, allowing hot water to run directly on it. Throw the Epsom salts in the water. After the tub is full, place the stone in the water. Soak your body in the warm water, knowing that as you do, the water is helping you draw new friends into your life.

Magical Cleansing Bath

    1 square piece of linen, about 2 x 2 inches
    Piece of string
    White sage

Rosemary

Sea salt

Tie equal portions of the ingredients into the square of linen. Whisper to the sachet your intent to cleanse yourself of all negative energies. Crush the ingredients in the sachet a bit with your hands. Place the sachet directly under the running water as you allow the bathtub to fill. As you soak in the bath, allow all of the negative things in your life to leave your spirit and flow into the water. When you emerge from the tub, be sure to bless your new self. It is proper to ask the Goddess to recycle the energies in the water and use them for positive purposes.

WATER CHARMS

Naturally occurring objects that are said to be empowered with magical properties manifest themselves in water as well as they do in the other elements. A sand dollar, for instance, is as potent a natural charm as a four-leaf clover.

Coral: The name coral has its roots in the Greek language. It translates literally to "daughter of the sea." An extremely protective talisman, coral has been accredited with driving away nightmares, harmful spirits, ghosts, theft, accidents, sterility, and violence. It is also credited with regulating menstruation.

Holey stones: Waves, sea creatures, and wind have been known to erode stone surfaces in such a way that a natural hole is created in the stone. These "holey stones" are very powerful in matters of protection. They are also said to be useful in healing rituals, as they absorb sickness and disease. An old wives' tale relates that looking through a holey stone will improve one's eyesight.

Mother-of-pearl: Mother-of-pearl is said to attract money as well as to protect. It is frequently used in ritual jewelry and placed on altars as a representative of water.

Pearls: Pearls have been thought for eons to be the tears of the Goddess. They are useful for attracting love and protection and improving one's luck.

Sand Dollars: The sand dollar is a potent natural good luck charm. A sand dollar is the skeleton of tiny sea creatures with the imprint of the five-pointed star upon them. In spell work, they are useful in matters involving protection, wisdom, and luck. The Water Witch sometimes uses a sand dollar as a representation of the pentacle on her altar.

Seaweed: The lore of seaweed was plentiful among the sailors of old. Seaweed was said to foretell the weather, promote friendships, and protect against fire or evil spirits. To divine the weather, keep a piece of seaweed beside the front door. If it shrivels, there will be warm weather. If it becomes moist, it will rain. To harness the friendship and protective aspects of seaweed, you only need to carry it. Burning seaweed produces a rich fertilizer that has been used in farming for centuries.

MOOD RING MAGIC

Mood ring magic is a particularly fun and unique form of magic that falls in the domain of water. Mood rings are thought to reflect the wearer's mood by virtue of their color. The stone in the ring picks up the energy channeled through the wearer's body and changes color accordingly. Scientists say this is due to our body heat, but we can tap this force for magical use regardless.

Here are some traditional mood stone colors and their meanings:

Black: Tense, nervous, overworked, harassed

Gray: Anxious, strained, nervous

Amber: Mixed emotions, nervous, unsettled

Green: Active, calm, normal mode

Blue-green: Semi-relaxed, active

Blue: Comfortable, happy, calm

Dark blue: Love, passion, romance

The odd thing about mood rings is while they work magically with all of the principles of water, you must not get them wet. The stone is comprised of liquid crystals, encased under a glass dome. If it gets wet, water can seep under the glass and cause damage to the crystals.

A mood ring can also be used on the altar as a representation of water. The goddess Tara was known for her skin changing color according to her mood, hence the mood ring has a symbolic link to her. Mood rings are widely available, and most are quite inexpensive to purchase.

The mood ring is a magical tool; it will do exactly what you tell it to do. When using a mood ring for magical purposes, be sure to state your intent clearly.

Pick-Me-Up

On a day when you are filled with happiness, it is a good idea to save some of that emotion in case you need a pick-me-up later, on a bad day. Put your mood ring on your right hand. Let it warm up to your emotions for a few minutes and then channel all of your happiness into the stone. Really pour it in there; it can hold as much as you can spare. When you are finished charging the ring, take it off and place it in a safe place. The mood stone will hold the emotion until you tell it to let it go. The next time you need a pick-me-up, wear the ring on your left hand and ask the stone to release to you the happiness you stored there earlier.

Be prepared for all of it to hit you at once. The mood stone is humanmade. It has no idea how to do anything other than exactly what you tell it. It will send the emotion all at once, so be sure you are in a place where it is okay to giggle.

Purge

If you are having a bad day and need to purge negative vibrations, you can do this with a mood ring as well. Place the ring on your right hand, and channel all of the emotion into the ring. Call upon the ring to cleanse itself—as it is ruled by the element of water, it is capable of doing so. Allow the ring forty-eight hours to remove all of the negative emotions before wearing it again. You may also place it in a bed of sea salt or sand if you are having particularly violent emotions.

Tapping Intuition

Wearing a mood ring while performing divination can be an experiment on its own. Try this, and record your findings in your divination journal. You may be surprised at the amount of knowledge this stone holds. It is also interesting to note the changes in a mood ring during ritual. It can truly be an enlightening experience.

SIMPLE WATER MAGIC

Some of the most effective types of magic are the easiest to perform. One method of water magic is to draw symbols on a sandy beach and wait for the waves to erase them and bring your spell to completion. You can use magical symbols or simple stick figures. You can also draw with soapstone or natural chalk and allow the rain to wash it away. Releasing things into a running stream is yet another method. The following spell is just one example of this type of magic. When it comes to simple ways to work with water, you are limited only by your imagination.

Note in a Bottle Spell

    1 glass bottle
    1 piece of paper
    A writing implement

Take the paper and write your wish upon it. Petition the goddess of the sea to bring this to you. Roll up the paper, slip it into the bottle, and cap it. Begin to count the waves rolling into shore, and on the ninth wave, cast the bottle far out into the sea. You can go about your day with confidence, knowing your wish will be fulfilled.

FLOATING CANDLES

Floating candles are used primarily to bring balance into the life of the spell caster. If you are working to achieve balance in a particular area of your life, you can choose a candle color that corresponds to your need. (See the beginning of chapter 13, "Fire Magic," for a list of candle colors and their correspondences.) Begin by charging the candle. Set it afloat in the water of your choice, and allow it to burn out. If working to banish something, you may light the candle and set it afloat in a slow-moving stream or creek. Watch from the shoreline as the candle moves away from you. If the flame goes out, don't worry—it has done its job.

If you are lucky enough to have a pond nearby that has lily pads, you can use these in rituals and spells by placing a tiny tealight candle on the surface of a lily pad and letting it float. This same technique can be utilized with any floating flower or plant.

WATER CORRESPONDENCES

Water is considered feminine and receptive.

Season: Winter

Magical Virtue: To Dare

Direction: West

Time of day: Dusk

Sense: Sight

Fluid: Tears

Power animals: Turtles, dolphins, whales, otters, frogs, seals, crabs, horses

Places of power: Beaches, harbors, piers, rivers, streams, creeks, waterfalls

Commonly associated colors: Blue and sea green

Linking items: Sand, shells, mood rings (symbolic link to Tara), seaweed, coral, mirrors

WATER STONES

Amethyst: The amethyst is one of the best-known magical stones. Said to cure drunkenness, a chunk of amethyst was often dropped into a goblet of wine. The amethyst is an intensely spiritual stone and is useful for opening the third eye, shifting consciousness, and increasing psychic awareness. It is said to have a calming influence. It also works well in beauty spells.

Aquamarine: The aquamarine is the stone of the Sea Witch. It is useful for increasing psychic awareness, cleansing, purifying, travel protection, and promoting peace and harmony.

Azurite: Another staple in the Water Witch's collection, this stone promotes psychic awareness and divination. It may also be used in healing spells.

Beryl: Beryl is the material used for true crystal balls. It can be worn to protect against foul weather or to call rain. It is said to calm arguments by allowing civil, intelligent debate.

Blue calcite: Blue calcite is useful for healing and purifying.

Blue lace agate: This stone promotes peace and happiness when worn or carried. It also absorbs stress. Blue lace agate has a calming influence on the household when placed about the home or worn as jewelry.

Celestite: Celestite absorbs stress, promotes healing, and helps the wearer express emotions. This stone is particularly useful in therapy settings.

Chalcedony: Chalcedony is another good stone in therapy settings. It also serves to guard against psychic attack and nightmares.

Jade: According to African belief, jade has the power to stimulate rain to fall. It is also used in fertility matters, as an attractant for good luck, and to attract love and friendship.

Lapis lazuli: Lapis lazuli is a stone of personal strength. When worn, it is said to improve one's mood, mental state, and eyesight and to calm the spirit by attracting universal forces of love. It also works well in matters pertaining to fidelity.

Lepidolite: Lepidolite is a stone of peace. Its relaxing vibrations are said to calm even the most hostile of tempers. It absorbs stress and anger.

Moonstone: The moonstone attracts love vibrations. It is also useful in fertility matters, protection, and increasing one's psychic vibrations.

Sapphire: Sacred to Apollo, the sapphire has been credited with increasing psychic awareness, love, protection, improving one's social life, and relieving anger.

Selenite: Selenite is used for boosting one's personal energy and deepening the bond between lovers.

Sodalite: Sodalite is another therapy stone. It is thought to relieve fear, stress, nervousness, anger, and mental imbalances.

WATER HERBS

Aloe: The aloe plant is healing and protective and is thought to improve one's luck.

Apple: The apple has long been used in love magic and represents immortality. It is also said to have healing properties. Apple seeds are said to increase luck when carried.

Apricot: The apricot is used to sweeten one's attitude and in love magic.

Aster: The aster is used in matters pertaining to love. The ancient Greeks considered the aster sacred to all the gods.

Bachelor buttons: The beautiful blue blossoms of the bachelor button flower have been used by single women for ages to attract love. To divine if an affair will be successful or not, pick a blossom and carry it in your pocket for twenty-four hours. If the flower is still fresh, the affair will grow. If it is withered, the affair will end.

Banana: The banana is said to work well in matters involving fertility, luck, and money.

Blackberry: Blackberry is one of the sacred foods of Lughnasadh. It is used to clear ailments such as boils, skin conditions, whooping cough, and rheumatism. The vines are thought to be protective. The leaves can draw prosperity and also serve as a mirror for negative vibrations.

Bladder wrack: Bladder wrack is a type of seaweed. It works well in matters involving protection and intuition.

Bleeding heart: A bleeding heart plant should never be placed indoors, because it has a reputation for creating negative vibrations. It has been said that the bleeding heart, when crushed, can foretell of love. However, when the blossom of a bleeding heart is crushed, it can stimulate anger. It is better to simply grow the plant outdoors—this will bring love your way.

Burdock: Burdock is extremely protective. It can be worn or placed around the home to ward off negativity.

Camellia: The camellia is thought to promote luck and prosperity.

Cardamom: Cardamom is used in love spells and for the promotion of lust. It is said to take effect quickly when placed in wine and consumed.

Catnip: Catnip is well known for its ability to please cats and facilitate a bond between owner and pet. It is also useful in spells for beauty, happiness, and love.

Chickweed: Chickweed is useful for both gaining and keeping love.

Coconut: The coconut is useful in spells involving purification, chastity, and protection. For protection, simply hang a coconut in the home.

Comfrey: Comfrey provides safety during travel when carried. The roots are frequently used in money magic.

Daffodil: The beautiful blossom of the daffodil is used to promote love, fertility, and luck. Old lore relates that it is bad luck to bring a single daffodil into the home—one should only bring a bunch.

Daisy: The daisy blossom is said to gift the wearer with special flirtation abilities. It attracts love. Placing the roots of a daisy plant under one's pillow is said to ensure dreams of one's future mate.

Elder: The elder has a distinguished reputation in the magical community. It is said to possess the powers of exorcism, healing, protection, and aiding sleep. It is known to be an extremely powerful talisman.

Elm: The elm protects against lightning, stabilizes energy, and attracts love. In Norse myths, the elm was said to be the source of the first woman.

Eucalyptus: Eucalyptus is an extremely powerful healing herb. It can also be carried for protection.

Feverfew: Carrying feverfew is said to protect against fevers.

Foxglove: Foxglove, a favorite among the fairy folk, can be planted in the garden for protection. Taking a foxglove into a home or onto a boat is not recommended, as it is thought to bring bad luck under such conditions.

Gardenia: Gardenias are useful for promoting spirituality, peace, and love. They are also thought to be healing.

Grape: Grapes represent fertility. The seeds are useful for spells involving mental processes.

Heather: Heather has a reputation for conjuring ghosts when burned. It is protective. It is commonly used with ferns in the making of rain-calling incense.

Hibiscus: The heady scent of the hibiscus induces love and lust.

Hyacinth: Hyacinth works well in matters involving love, protection, and happiness.

Iris: The iris is a special herb due to its beauty. The blossom is thought to absorb negative vibrations. It also attracts wisdom.

Jasmine: Jasmine blossoms draw love and money and heighten intuition.

Lady's mantle: Lady's mantle is used primarily in matters of love.

Lady's slipper: Lady's slipper is used primarily in matters of protection.

Larkspur: Larkspur is protective. It has been said that the flowers keep away ghosts and poisonous creatures.

Lemon: Lemons are often used in curses, as the juice is thought to sour situations. However, lemons are also cleansing and are known to attract love and friendship.

Lilac: Lilac is known to drive away negative influences.

Lily: The blossoms of the lily are protective. Lilies also possess the ability to break any spells cast upon a person by another.

Lotus: The blossoms of the lotus are protective. This flower is sacred in the East.

Lucky hand: The root of an orchid known as lucky hand is thought to protect as well as to attract money, jobs, and luck.

Mesquite: The wood of mesquite is used in healing spells.

Mimosa: Mimosa is a cleansing herb. It also attracts love.

Morning glory: The morning glory root can be used as a substitute for High John the Conqueror root. The blossoms bring peace and happiness.

Myrrh: Myrrh is healing and protective and magnifies the power of other additives in sachets or incenses.

Myrtle: Myrtle is capable of drawing love, peace, and money. It is often used in fertility rites.

Orchid: The orchid is known to attract love. In the past, it was used in an aphrodisiac potion.

Orris root: Orris root is a primary ingredient in love-attracting potions, powders, and sachets. It also has a protective quality.

Pansy: Pansy flowers are thought to draw love. Picking a pansy flower on a day of good weather is thought to bring rain.

Passion flower: The passion flower is known to induce peaceful vibrations and calm arguments.

Pear: Pear wood is often used in magical wands. The fruit is thought to induce love and lust.

Periwinkle: Periwinkle induces passion when sprinkled near the bed. It is thought to attract money and good fortune. One should never pick periwinkle from a grave—to do so allows the ghost of the person buried there to haunt one's dreams for a full year.

Plum: The fruit of the plum tree is said to maintain and attract loving vibrations. The wood is thought to ward off evil.

Plumeria: The delightful fragrance of the plumeria flower has made it a favorite offering of many Witches. It can also be used to attract love.

Poppy: Poppy seeds placed under one's pillow are said to promote a good night's rest. They are also said to attract love, money, and fertility. Superstition warns against bringing the poppy indoors, as it was thought to cause illness.

Rose: The rose is extremely powerful in love spells. The blossoms also calm turbulent emotions and promote harmony.

Spearmint: Spearmint is an extremely powerful healing herb. It is also said to promote intellect and attract love.

Spikenard: Spikenard is thought to promote fidelity and good health.

Strawberry: Strawberry leaves, when carried by pregnant women, are thought to ease aches and pains. The fruit is thought to attract love and good fortune.

Sugar cane: Sugar cane draws love and good luck. When burned, it cleanses the area, allowing only sweet things to remain.

Sweetpea: Sweetpea blossoms attract friends and bolster courage.

Tansy: Tansy is used as an ant repellent. When carried, it is thought to increase one's lifespan.

Thyme: Thyme has a decidedly dark history, as it is associated with murder. The lingering scent of the thyme plant can be found at sights where violent deaths occurred. Despite this negative reputation, thyme is a cleansing and healing herb. When placed beneath one's pillow, it is thought to aid sleep.

Valerian: Valerian is an energy booster and is cleansing and protective. It is also thought to attract love.

Violet: Violets bring relief from hauntings. They promote good luck and peace. However, only bring violet blossoms indoors by the bunch, as it is thought to be unlucky to do otherwise.

Willow: The willow tree has a long association with death. It works well in matters of transformation, healing, love, and protection. However, never tell a willow your secrets, as it is known to repeat them to the wind.

Wintergreen: Wintergreen is healing and protective and is thought to be able to break curses. It promotes good health when carried.

Yarrow: Yarrow is very useful in potions and various infusions. Yarrow tea is said to cure baldness, cleanse objects for magical use, and improve psychic powers. It also helps regulate menstruation.

8

WATER GODS AND GODDESSES

TARA

The Hindu sea goddess Tara rescued sailors in peril. She was the mother of the Buddha three times over. Today she is seen more as an aspect of Kali instead of the goddess in her own right that she once was. It is said that she is the incarnation of purity. Her name means "the star." It is also said that she was born from a tear falling from the eye of Avalokitesvara, which formed a lake on Earth. A lotus emerged from the water and blossomed to reveal Tara.

Tara has three eyes, one of which is in the center of her forehead. She is mostly seen as slender and beautiful, with long, golden hair and blue eyes. She was known for her ability to change skin colors. When angered she would be either blue or yellow. When calm she was green or white. When red she represented love.

Tara is known as a goddess of compassion and was once thought of as the savior goddess. She is renowned for her ability to help others see things clearly and maintain a stable path. She is a fierce protector. Tara is the goddess of the moon. Legends relate that at one point she was told that in order to further develop her process of enlightenment, she must incarnate as a man. Tara refused and made a vow to only incarnate in female form. Thereafter she was known as the Moon of Wisdom.

Tara's worship spread wide, even into the Polynesian areas. Evidence suggests that her worship is ancient.

The Polynesian Tara is a sea goddess, renowned for her beauty. In fact, she is said to be so beautiful that if you catch sight of her, your gaze will remain transfixed.

POSEIDON

Poseidon is the Greek god of the water, ruler of the seas. However, his power was much more complex and encompasses more than the sea. The son of Titans Cronus and Rhea, he was thought to be the force behind earthquakes and was closely linked to horses and bulls. His Roman counterpart is Neptune.

Poseidon was described as having white hair, a long white beard, and fierce blue eyes. He carried a trident (a three-pronged spear) that was gifted to him by the Cyclops when the Olympians overthrew the Titans. He rode about in a golden chariot, which was said to be shell-shaped. Poseidon was not the only water deity of the ancient Greeks, but he was the one in command.

In certain myths, it was Poseidon who coupled with Demeter when she was disguised as a colt. Poseidon transformed himself into a stallion, and together they had two children, one of which was the horse Areion. In this aspect, Poseidon was known as Hippios and was worshipped as the protector of horsemen. The very first horse, Sciphius, was born of the Earth and the seed of Poseidon. The name Poseidon means "husband." It is asserted that Poseidon was married to his sister Demeter and was therefore husband of the Earth itself.

In one legend, Poseidon was said to have created the horse in an effort to win the city of Athens as his own. (Other myths assert that his gift to the Athenians was the spring of Acropolis.) Athena gifted the people with the olive tree, which was considered at that time to be more useful; hence she won the city. Poseidon was outraged and flooded the land. Later, as his temper subsided, the water slowly withdrew. Yet, he retained the reputation of being Athena's rival.

Poseidon was one of three brothers upon Olympus. After the war with the Titans, he was assigned rulership of the sea, while his brother Zeus was assigned the sky and his brother Hades the Underworld. The realm of Earth was common ground.

Poseidon was a formidable god. Easily irritated and highly temperamental, he was known to send violent waves at those who displeased him. He was responsible for diverting Odysseus from his route to Ithaca by causing trouble in this manner. Poseidon went after Odysseus as revenge, because Odysseus had blinded and taunted Poseidon's son, Polyphemos. After many years of misfortune, Odysseus finally planted an oar in the sand and dedicated a shrine to Poseidon to appease his anger.

Poseidon was also responsible for the release of a sea creature upon Andromeda, because her mother, Cassiopeia, was a stupid, vain woman who had dared to compare Andromeda's beauty to that of the sea nymphs.

Ovid relates that it was Poseidon who covered the Earth with the great flood. It was determined by Zeus that, after Pandora opened the box releasing evil into the world, the world should begin anew, without these influences. So he called upon his brother Poseidon to immerse the Earth in water. Poseidon opened all natural dams, overflowed all riverbanks, and sent violent waves crashing upon the soil.

Poseidon was also the force that caused earthquakes. He would strike his trident upon rocks and cause the world to burst open, forming natural springs for fresh water to surface.

As terrible as Poseidon could be, he was also irresistible to women. His many dalliances produced hundreds of offspring before he married Amphitrite the Nereid. Amphitrite was thought of as the mother of all seals and dolphins. In order to persuade her to marry him, Poseidon sent one of her dolphin children to plead his case.

Poseidon was also bisexual, a rather common theme in classical mythology that is underexplored today. One legend recounts the story of Poseidon and Pelops. Pelops was the son of King Tantalus. King

Tantalus invited all of the Olympians to a feast, only there was one problem—he had no food. He thought to trick them and test their intuitive powers at the same time. He cut his son Pelops into pieces, boiling him in a stew. The Olympians were not fooled. Only Demeter, who was distraught over her daughter's disappearance, tasted the food. Tantalus was immediately destroyed, and the Olympians went about restoring life to his son. Pelops came back to life more beautiful than he had been before.

Poseidon, upon seeing the young man's beauty, was lovestruck. He carried Pelops in his chariot to Mount Olympus to serve as his lover and cupbearer. The other gods, still burned by the actions of Tantalus, returned Pelops to Earth. Poseidon allowed him to go but gifted him with enough riches to live his life in comfort.

Later in life, Pelops himself felt the pangs of love and asked Poseidon to help him win a race so that he could marry Hippodameia. Poseidon graciously gave the boy a chariot led by immortal winged horses. When Pelops' opponents drew close, they had unfortunate accidents and subsequently died. Thus, Pelops won the hand of Hippodameia.

The gorgon Medusa figures into Poseidon's myths in the most tragic of ways. Legends relate that Poseidon came upon the beautiful Medusa in Athena's temple, where she served as high priestess. He was so overcome by her beauty that he seduced her right then and there. Athena, who was already jealous of Medusa's stunning beauty and considered Poseidon her archrival, was outraged. She turned Medusa into a hideous beast, with snakes for hair. Later, when Perseus cut off Medusa's head, the winged horse Pegasus sprang forth from the blood. Poseidon was reputed to be the father of Pegasus.

Poseidon was known to bestow the gift of shapeshifting on others. He was said to have gifted this ability to the young woman Caenis, transforming her into a male warrior, at her request. In this aspect, he was compared to Proteus, the old man of the sea. At Poseidon's command, Caenis became Caeneus, a formidable warrior. Caeneus was so empowered by his role as a warrior after a lifetime spent as a female that he walked into town one day, planted his spear in the ground, and commanded the people to worship his spear as a god. Zeus was enraged at this blasphemy and sent a hoard of Centaurs to destroy Caeneus. As Caeneus died, he shapeshifted back into female form.

Fishermen and sailors tried to win Poseidon's favors with offerings and prayers. All too often, they failed to satisfy him and met with watery deaths.

Poseidon also figures into the legends of Atlantis. Plato asserted that Atlantis was a large island in the Atlantic Ocean. Because the people of Atlantis were thought to have evolved into spiritually ugly and war-mongering people, Zeus gave Poseidon the go-ahead to cover the land with water, wiping them from the face of the Earth.

The ancient Romans honored Neptune (Poseidon) on July 23, a day when water was at its lowest level. The Hellenic calendar marks the month of Poseidon as November 17 through December 15. Every few years there would be an extra month added to the calendar year. This month was known as the second Poseidon.

YEMAYA

Yemaya is known as the "great mother," the mother of the Orishas. Yemaya is the Orisha who rules the oceans and seas in Santerían traditions and Yoruban myths. She is credited with giving birth to all streams, springs, rivers, and creeks. Not only is she the mother of all Orishas, she is the mother of all water.

Yemaya is said to live in the oceans. Offerings are left for her along the shorelines, where the morning tides float them out into her arms. Fish are sacred to Yemaya; they are never given as an offering to her. Her favorite offerings are yams, watermelon, molasses, black-eyed peas, soap, perfume, jewelry, and grains. She is sometimes summoned by the ritualistic shaking of special gourd rattles.

Yemaya's colors are blue, white, and silver, and her number is seven. Her day is Saturday. She enjoys crystals, pearls, and mother-of-pearl. The cowrie shell is sacred to her. Her primary feast days are September 7, February 2, and December 31. She is a water deity; it is the skirts of Yemaya that form the fabric of the seas. Her hair is said to be the stars. In her honor, practitioners celebrate her feast days by wearing seven skirts composed of blue, white, and silver tones.

In addition to water, Yemaya also rules the moon, dreams, reproduction, secrets, wisdom, and seashells. She is instrumental in helping people discover their past lives and other tasks of that nature, such as developing psychic skills. She is a fierce protector and the ruler of retribution.

Yemaya maintains a close connection to Isis and the Virgin Mary. The African elemental known as Mama Wata (Mama Water) is her kin. In Voodoo, she is seen as Lasiren, a mermaid. She has many aspects to her personality. They are as follows:

Yemaya Olokun: Olokun is the deep water aspect. In this capacity she is said to rule over all things that lie at the bottom of the oceans and to guard secrets. Olokun is thought to be a temptress.

Yemaya Okuti: In this aspect we find the destructive side of Yemaya. Okuti is known for her powerful magic, vengeful temper, and fierce warrior prowess. We find her among rocks that break water, such as at the bottom of a waterfall or along a coastline.

Yemaya Acuaro: In this aspect we find the healing nature of Yemaya. This is also the aspect used for breaking bad luck or hexes and spiritual cleansing. Acuaro lives where fresh water meets with salt water.

Yemaya Achabba: Achabba is a serious, strict aspect of Yemaya. She is wise and is known to discipline her followers if needed.

Yemaya Mayalewo: Mayalewo lives in the rainforests and water bodies that lie in wooded areas. In this capacity Yemaya is regarded as peaceful and solitary.

Yemaya Awoyo: This is the oldest of all of Yemaya's aspects. Awoyo is seen as wise, caring, honorable, and loving. She is a powerful warrior.

Yemaya Oquette: Oquette is another destructive aspect of Yemaya and is said to be violent at times. She serves to remind us that as mother she can both create and destroy life.

Yemaya Asseu: Asseu is the death aspect of Yemaya and is said to live in polluted waters, where she receives the bodies of the dead.

Curiously, one legend speaks of Yemaya's dislike for the Orisha Oya. It seems that long ago, Yemaya ruled over cemeteries and Oya ruled the oceans. Yemaya longed for the beauty of the sparkling waves instead of the eternal death all around her. To accomplish the switch, she bragged to Oya about how beautiful her home was. Oya spoke of how unsatisfied she was with the ocean as a home. Yemaya took Oya to the gate, but would not let her in. She further bragged about how extravagant her lodgings were. Oya was enchanted and believed her.

Yemaya said she would switch places with her to let her see how wonderful the place was, and Oya agreed. Once Oya had taken up residence in the gateway for the dead, she realized that Yemaya's former home was not all she had made it out to be. When Oya tried to change places again, Yemaya refused. Due to this episode, the two Orishas are never fed at the same time, and their altars must be kept separate from each other. It is further suggested that the practice of keeping their food separate on the altar was born from Oya's aversion to ram, a customary food for Yemaya.

Yemaya, as the mother of life, is the caretaker of her sister Ochun's children. She raised Chango as well. After Chango's parents threw him out of their house, Yemaya took him in and raised him as her son. Over the years, Chango grew up and moved off on his own, conveniently forgetting his tragic childhood. Chango turned into a rabble-rouser and a womanizer. After years of this lifestyle, the jaded Chango met up with Yemaya at a party, not remembering who she was. He was drawn to her beauty and tried to seduce her. Yemaya decided to teach Chango a lesson he would not forget.

Yemaya feigned interest in Chango and led him out to a boat. Promising ecstasy, she had Chango (who was afraid of water) untie the docking ropes and get in. The two drifted so far out into the ocean that they could no longer see the shore. Frightened, Chango demanded that they go closer to the shoreline. In response, Yemaya dove over the side of the boat, slipping smoothly into the water. She began sending strong waves to rock the little boat and turned it over. Chango righted the boat and climbed back in. Terrified, he begged Yemaya to save him. She told him she would do so, but under one condition. He must remember to respect his mother. At once, Chango remembered who she was, and agreed. It was said that after this lesson he was still a womanizer, but a much more respectful one.

OCHUN

Yemaya's sister Ochun is the Orisha who rules over fresh water. She also rules love, beauty, money, happiness, and dance and is thought to be quite promiscuous. Her blessings rain down upon those who endeavor to make the world more beautiful—these blessings are said to have no limits. Her colors are yellow and gold, due to her connection with money. She shares Saturday as her special day with her sister Yemaya. Her number is five. She has a special fondness for mirrors and peacock feathers.

Ochun is a temptress with a fondness for trickery. It is said that no man or Orisha could resist her. Ochun wanted to learn the art of divination. Obatala was the only one who knew the secrets of divination, but he refused to teach her. One day Obatala went to the river to bathe. Elegba passed by and, seeing an opportunity, snatched up Obatala's clothes and took them home. Ochun was picking flowers nearby when she heard Obatala's bellowing. Obatala asked Ochun to retrieve his clothing, so that he would not be disgraced. She extracted a promise from him first: he must agree to teach her the art of divination. Obatala agreed.

Ochun prepared for her meeting with Elegba by painting her body with glistening honey. She wore only five yellow scarves around her waist. She followed Elegba's footprints to his home. When Elegba answered the door, his gaze remained transfixed on Ochun. She stood in the doorway with her arms akimbo and demanded he return Obatala's clothing at once. Elegba, so enchanted by her beauty that he could not think clearly, could only reply with mumbles about mating with her. Eventually, Elegba and Ochun reached a compromise, for she returned with Obatala's clothing. Obatala kept his word and taught Ochun the art of divination.

Another example of Ochun's sensual enticement is the legend of Ogun. Ogun, the blacksmith, went into the forest, determined to live his life alone. When he did, the natural force of creation came to a screeching halt. Knowing he was needed in the world, Ochun went to a nearby clearing wearing her five yellow scarves and carrying a gourd of honey. Instead of trying to talk Ogun into coming out, she began to dance. Ogun was enraptured. In a daze, he walked slowly out of the forest and into the clearing. Ochun then smeared honey upon his lips and began to dance back to civilization. Ogun followed and went back to work.

Although Ochun is a temptress, known for her sexuality, she is also known to help in matters involving fidelity. As the goddess of both love and intimacy, she is often invoked by those wishing to be married or those with problems within their marriage.

Ochun shares the responsibility of reproduction and childbirth with her sister Yemaya, but allows Yemaya to raise her children. Ochun also reigns over cleansings before crowning ceremonies (a rite in which the practitioner makes contact with his or her personal Orisha). Another of Ochun's aspects lives in sacred drums and calls the spirits and Orishas to ceremonies.

Ochun is said to be so enchanting that if offended, she will kill while smiling. It is rare for her to become so offended, but she demands her due respect.

Ochun demands respect for women, too. In one legend, the male Orishas held a secret meeting. Ochun asked if she could attend but was refused entry. Enraged, she made all females barren and threw the natural world balance out of sync. The male Orishas were worried, so they invited Ochun to their meeting. She was so angry, she refused. The male Orishas had to cajole her into attending and offered her gifts of gold and copper. She still refused. Finally, they offered her honey. Ochun forgave them and turned the women fertile again.

GANGA

Ganga is the Hindu goddess of the river that was named after her—the Indian river Ganga. Because this is the most sacred of water bodies in India, she is a goddess of great importance. On her banks, the people find both life and death.

Ganga is depicted as a fair-skinned woman, wearing a white crown. She sits upon a crocodile and holds a lily blossom in her right hand. In her left hand, she holds a lute. Legend states that she was born from the sweat of Vishnu's feet.

In order for Ganga to fall from heaven to Earth, she had to do it in three installments, so as not to flood the world. Eventually, the water flowed in separate directions, creating other rivers. Ganga also flows in the heavens, on Earth, and in the Underworld.

Her worshippers believe that touching her waters, looking upon them, and saying her sacred name will cleanse one of their sins and bestow the greatest of blessings. It is further believed that disposing of human remains in her waters will bless the dead and lead them to salvation. Because of this, cremation sites line her banks, and ashes and bones float in her waters.

Ganga's water is so sacred that it is used to compel people to tell the truth. It is said that no Hindu would dare lie while holding her in their hand.

Parvati felt that Ganga made absolution too readily available and that as a result, it would no longer have any meaning. Shiva disagreed and offered to show Parvati how gaining salvation was not as easy as one may think. He lay down on the shore and pretended to be dead. Parvati pretended to be his widow, crying loudly. Everyone tried to console her. To all of their efforts she replied, "I dreamt of Lord Shiva. He told me he would restore life to my husband's body if a person who had been cleansed of all sins in the river Ganga would but touch the body. But if that person had not truly been cleansed, he would die." All the onlookers gasped. No one was so sure of their salvation that they were willing to risk death.

All of a sudden, the best-known rabble-rouser and drunkard in the area came forth. He told the widow that he was a huge sinner, but had faith in the cleansing of the Ganga. Surely he would be able to help her restore life to her husband. He bathed in her waters and touched the body. Lord Shiva stood and said to the startled crowd, "Only one of you here today had the faith and repentance needed to be cleansed. The rest of you simply got wet." Parvati was pleased to see that absolution goes hand in hand with faith and belief.

SEDNA

Sedna is the Native American Sea Woman from the Arctic regions. She is believed to live beneath the ocean and guard all sea creatures, especially seals.

Sedna was not always immortal; she began her life as human. Her legends state that she lived with her father. Sedna was very beautiful, and very vain as well. She thought she was too beautiful to marry just anyone. Dozens of suitors came by asking for her hand in marriage, but she refused them all.

One day her father told her he could not afford to support her anymore and that she must marry—quickly. He told her she would marry the next suitor that came for her. Sedna said nothing; she simply continued to stare at her reflection in the pond.

The next suitor to arrive was dressed richly and carried many pelts. His face was hidden, but the father paid no attention. He went up to the suitor and said, "If you seek a bride, I have a beautiful daughter. She will make a good wife." The suitor said he would take her.

Sedna did not want to go, and they had to force her into the man's kayak for the journey to her new home. When they arrived on his island, Sedna found he had no hut or dwelling in place. Then her husband finally revealed his face. He was not a man at all but a trickster raven. She only had bare rocks to live on and raw fish to eat. She was miserable.

She spent her days crying and calling out to her father to come save her. Her father caught her cries upon the cold winds. Feeling guilty, he undertook the task to save his daughter. He loaded up his kayak and went off to find her. Upon his arrival, Sedna hugged him and jumped into the kayak, and the two made haste to be gone from the horrid island before the raven's return. They had been paddling for a while when Sedna noticed a black speck in the sky, coming their way. It was her husband, the raven.

Raven harassed the two, with the father trying to beat him off with a paddle. Finally, he started to flap his wings so ferociously that a great storm began to churn. The tiny kayak almost capsized. The father, scared out of his mind, threw Sedna over the side of the kayak and told the raven, "Here is your wife. Now leave me be!"

Sedna desperately clung to the side of the boat. Her body quickly became numb from the icy water. Her father, thinking only of himself, beat upon her fingers with an oar. She begged him to stop, but he was so frightened that he would not. Finally, he succeeded in chopping her fingers off, whereupon she slipped quietly into the sea.

Sedna did not realize that her husband's powers would affect her, but they did. As her fingers drifted to the bottom of the sea, they turned into seals and swam around her. Sedna was so outraged at what had happened to her that she did not drown. Instead, she embraced her new kingdom and became the Sea Woman. When Sedna is angry, she causes violent storms and massive waves.

It was said that the only known way to calm her was to dive to the bottom of the sea and brush her hair. Sedna always took pride in her beauty, and without fingers, she could no longer groom herself. She would hold all of the sea creatures under water until this was done, which threatened the people with starvation. Because she is the mother of all that lives in the water and does not look favorably upon humankind, it is said that the spirits of the animals she provides to the people stay with their bodies for three days to make sure that none of her laws are being broken. After that time period, they return to Sedna and report their findings.

Sedna finally had her revenge. Her father, so wracked with guilt that he could not sleep, lay down at the shoreline and begged her forgiveness. As he did, he cried himself to sleep. Sedna sent the tide and brought him out to the deep sea, where he drowned.

KANALOA

Kanaloa is the Hawaiian god of the sea. He is the eternal companion of Kane (who rules over fresh water) and is thought to be his shadow side. Kane is the father god of all Hawaiians. Kanaloa is known to have many aspects, the main representation being that of a giant octopus. In human form, he was described as being very tall and fair-skinned.

One legend describes Kane and Kanaloa as exact opposites. While Kane is the creator god, Kanaloa is the destroyer. The legend states that Kanaloa is responsible for human mortality. Kane drew a figure of a man in the dirt, and Kanaloa followed suit. Kane's creation came to life, but Kanaloa's did not. In a fit of rage, Kanaloa spitefully cursed all of humankind to eventually die.

Kanaloa was the first leader of spirits that were placed upon the Earth. These spirits had been thrown out of the heavens by the other gods. They were refused the right to drink awa, a drink similar to tea, so they rebelled. They were eventually defeated and cast into the Underworld. Kanaloa became associated as the ruler of the dead in this manner. However, he is mentioned in ancient Hawaiian chants as the deepest waters of the sea, that is, "fished up from the depths of Kanaloa." In that phrase we find where Kanaloa was originally linked to the dead.

In fact, many of his legends place Kanaloa as Kane's opposite and continually causing strife. It is important to note that this aspect of his personality could have been clouded by Christian missionaries equating him with their figure of Satan. The adversarial personality is only one aspect of Kanaloa. In other stories we find him to be protective, healing, and benevolent. Instead of fighting Kane, he was his friend, and both were awa drinkers. It was their main source of food. Kanaloa was known to be a great healer and knew all of the secrets of medicine. He traveled the land with Kane providing springs of fresh water and stocked fish ponds for the people. Fishermen invoke Kanaloa to this day for protection. The tides are said to roll in and out according to Kanaloa's breathing. The direction of west is thought of as the "much traveled road of Kanaloa" in Hawaiian folklore. He is also thought to rule the south.

PART THREE
AIR

9

THE PATH OF THE AIR WITCH

The path of the Air Witch is one of constant mental stimulation and expression. As poets, writers, actors, and dreamers, Air Witches walk the line of creativity. The wind is the soliloquy of life; every thought and sound transports itself through the air.

Seen as flaky and airheaded by some, the strength of the Air Witch lies in her intelligence, not her common sense. She walks around with her head in the clouds. Too often she suffers from "foot in mouth" disease. She seems to have an uncanny knack for saying the wrong thing at the wrong time. Uncomfortable with silence, the Air Witch is content to chatter on aimlessly. She is well-known for making people laugh and smile, even when she is on their last nerve.

A key strength of the master of the wind is her flexibility. The Air Witch always allows room to change her mind and to bend with the wind. She considers that she is never fully "done"; she is a work in progress. Just as you cannot capture the wind, you cannot pin down an Air Witch to one viewpoint for too long. She refuses to stagnate by accepting anything to be true all of the time. She is inquisitive, bubbly, and bright, and can inspire others to reach higher, try harder, and give a goal their best shot. Air Witches make wonderful cheerleaders.

On the flip side, the happy-go lucky Air Witch is not one you want to anger. Her fury rouses quickly, and she usually possesses a nasty temper. An Air Witch will not mince words with you—she will cut straight to the bone. Once her outburst is over, she is usually no longer mad. Five minutes after her tantrum, she has no idea why anyone is angry with her.

Due to her flighty nature, the Air Witch has an easy time letting go of the past. She can overcome the most tragic of life's situations. She will be changed, but she will quickly move on. She is truly like the wind. Because of this, she tends to make bad judgments. She does not always think things through fully before taking action.

The Air Witch thrives on change and new beginnings. Nothing will excite her more than moving to a new location, getting a new job, meeting new people, or going on a vacation. She often changes her style throughout her lifetime, including favorite colors, textures, and even foods.

Her thirst for knowledge is unquenchable and tends to get her in trouble. She keeps an open mind and is willing to see alternate viewpoints. The Air Witch is known to incorporate many different belief systems into her own personal view.

Among the many quirks of Air Witches, claustrophobia rates unusually high in their ranks. The Air Witch cannot stand the thought of being trapped in a place with limited air. Scuba diving or the like is a rare activity for an Air Witch, as she fears suffocation above all else.

The Air Witch's home is normally very clean. She can be extremely picky about dirt and dust. However, when entering the home of an Air Witch, you are apt to find many projects in various stages just sitting around waiting for her to complete them. The windy Air Witch does not always have the stamina needed to complete what she starts. It makes perfect sense to her to do the laundry and then fold it and stack it, without ever putting it away. She is easily distracted.

The home of an Air Witch is usually neutral-toned and light, with many windows. She frequently will have an abundance of houseplants and overstocked cabinets filled with convenience foods and sugary junk. It's no wonder Air Witches have weak teeth, as they usually have an inexhaustible sweet tooth.

If you are friends with an Air Witch, prepare to be inspired. She wants her friends and loved ones to achieve their desired level of success just as badly as they do. The Air Witch gives herself to her friends selflessly. However, once betrayed, she will never trust that person again. The Air Witch is all about movement, and she refuses to get caught in other people's hang-ups. She is not one to give second chances. Because of her willingness to please, and the fact that she strives to make all things just, she may actually say that she will grant someone a second chance and then try to, but rarely can she do it in her heart. Once trust is gone for her, it is gone. She moves on.

The Air Witch is optimistic and energetic. She always starts off strong, even if her efforts dwindle later. It is the same in all areas of her life. Her first magic is the strongest, and she usually instinctually knows her element instantly. The only part of her life where this factor does not enter into the equation is in the case of first love. Once a relationship is over for her, it is over. The Air Witch does not live in the past, but in the present. The love she has now is the only one that matters.

The Air Witch can maintain her stamina to complete a project if she perceives it to be a challenge. Telling an Air Witch that she can't do something is a sure way to see to it that she does. However, if she guesses that she is being manipulated in this fashion, she will erupt into a tantrum. She despises manipulative games and tends to see through them quickly, due to her own manipulative nature.

Because the air blankets the Earth and water, the Air Witch frequently has a large ego. She sees herself as above others and counts on her sister elements to keep this ego in check. A key lesson for the windy ones is learning that they are not the only creatures that count. However, this position also grants the Air Witch the ability to see all sides of a situation. She is very just.

The Air Witch has a hard time showing the proper respect due to others in authoritative positions, because she does not see anyone as superior to her. She is strong and fiercely independent. Due to the placement of her element, she can also be very derisive in her humor when it is pointed at herself. She does not take herself too seriously and finds much to laugh about. Compliments thrill her, but expressions of thanks tend to embarrass her. She is usually very social and has a wide network of friends. Happy and upbeat as a rule, she can allow herself to become depressed when she does not meet her goals. She is very hard on herself.

The Air Witch can be highly superstitious. She accepts that not all things exist within the scope of the human senses. Within the realm of air lie the keys to invisibility, sound, thinking, communication, creativity, weather, the dead, and ghosts, just to name a few. It is no wonder that the Air Witch seems to operate on a different level—she does. Considering the multitude of things she hosts in her space, she is usually adept at reading signs and omens. The Air Witch is well schooled in sky divination and portents or harbingers of luck.

The Air Witch specializes magically in spirits, ghosts, invisible beings, travel, inspiration, dreams, wishes, creativity, and changes. She often has a special affinity for Ouija, pendulums, and storm and weather magic. She tends to be unconventional and does things that are considered taboo among many Witches, such as blowing out her candles, using items that don't biodegrade, and so on.

Whereas the Water Witch has a talent for divination and the intuitive arts, the Air Witch has a talent for necromancy and clairaudience. The Air Witch is usually well trained in aromatherapy, meditation, and pain-management breathing techniques.

Water rules creation, earth rules rebirth, and air rules the cross over a threshold—in other words, the gates of death. The Air Witch has a decidedly dark side and a complex character. Her focus is more on the death side of nature, due to her realm, which includes death, along with sustaining life. You can only survive a few minutes without air, but if you breathe the wrong air, such as poisonous gas, you will die immediately. Air brings disease, death, and destruction side by side with life.

The Air Witch is very insightful in the realm of past-life discovery, because time itself belongs to her element as well.

At the same time, air cannot create or re-create life on its own. An Air Witch needs her sister element earth to recycle her winds (through plant life) and water and fire to aid growth. Air Witches may have trouble in the areas relating to menstruation and reproduction. Other potential health problems include spinal conditions or a bad back, asthma, or hearing loss.

Air rules the mental processes, and Air Witches often have a few problems in that area. They are frequently nervous, jittery types, prone to panic attacks. In nature, we find crosswinds, tornadoes, and hurricanes—it seems that wind itself has an insane pattern. The Air Witch is the same. When angered or hurt, she can easily cross the line into the realm of madness. She may entertain notions of revenge, but since she changes her mind constantly, she rarely sees them through. The windy Air Witch is easily depressed and is known to go into a funk over the smallest of things. However, she rarely stays down for long.

The winds are important to the element of air, but they are not the element itself. However, the two are inseparable. The element of air encircles the globe; it is the atmosphere. Every sunrise and sunset takes place in its domain. In this manner we discover how the Air Witch connects to the earthly elements—she incarnates the aura of them, the same way the atmosphere is the aura of the planet. Often, the Air Witch is the catalyst needed to create a change. She is mysterious and unpredictable.

THE DARK SIDE OF THE AIR WITCH

Do not threaten an Air Witch or what she holds dear, as she is fiercely protective. When she feels threatened, she goes into overdrive and absolutely will not rest until the threat is destroyed completely. She rarely practices defensive magic, preferring instead to allow those who dare to attack face their karmic backlash instead, as she is always willing to accept hers. She can be manipulative in this manner and may not even realize it.

Usually well versed in destructive magic, the Air Witch takes all acts of magic deadly seriously. She insists that a simple blessing carries the same power behind it as a two-hour ritual. When angered, the emotion simply has to run its course, and that course can be decidedly ugly. Just as air feeds fire, the Air Witch feeds her own inner fire when she is angry. She stews and will not move beyond her anger until she is ready. Once she is, it is much easier for her to simply remove the influence from her life entirely. She will cut people out of her life without a second thought.

AIR WITCH LORE

Thunder

Symbolized in myths by powerful and revered deities such as Thor, Hera, and Zeus, thunderbolts are also perceived as the spirits of the air. Once thought of as expressions of the gods' anger and universally feared, thunder and lightning are portrayed as benevolent in many myths.

In Native American beliefs, thunder and lightning are represented by the Thunderbirds. It was thought that lightning would flash as the birds opened their eyes and that the thunder was created from the flapping of their wings. The birds were thought to be gigantic.

The thunderbird was thought of as benevolent by most tribes, but a few believed it to be unlucky. For example, the Winnebago tribe saw the thunderbird as a harbinger of war.

A common misconception is that the thunderbird was a man-eater and as such was feared. The thunderbird was simply a nature spirit personified in extremely large proportions. The piasa is an example of a man-eating mythical bird. The two birds are often confused.

According to the lore of the Lakota tribe, the greatest of the thunderbirds is named Wakinyan Tanka. Wakinyan Tanka lives high on a mountain. He detests things that are dirty. It is said that he dwells in a massive tipi and rests in a nest of human bones. It is in that nest that the egg of the thunderbird is hatched.

The Lakotas believe that there are four thunderbirds, each guarding a specific direction. The western thunderbird is represented by the color black. Likewise, the eastern thunderbird is represented by yellow, the southern by white, and the northern by red. Thunderbirds naturally move in a widdershins direction and are thought to be clumsy, awkward creatures.

Thunderbirds are the guardians of humans and truth. These great spirits of the air are credited with saving humankind during the great flood and fighting with the demonic creatures that caused the flood in order to obtain humanity's continued life. They are fiercely protective.

In Japanese creation myths, there were eight forms of thunder. All were born from the dead body of Izanami, the female creator spirit. Izanagi, her husband and brother and the creator god, came upon Izanami's body in a ghastly state of decomposition. He saw the eight thunder gods living in her body. Great Thunder was in her head, Fire Thunder in her breast, Black Thunder in her womb, Rending Thunder in her abdomen, Young Thunder in her left hand, Rumbling Thunder in her left foot, Earth Thunder in her right hand, and Couchant Thunder in her right foot. Izanagi ran away from the sight out of fear. Later, the thunder gods served as a protective force for Izanagi in the Underworld.

Bells, Wind Chimes, and Musical Lore

All around the globe, bells are credited with removing and dispelling negative energies and entities, due to their high-frequency vibrations. However, bells can also summon fairies, entities, and spirits.

A bell has a natural polarity present in its very shape. The outer skirt of the bell represents the divine feminine, while the clapper represents the divine masculine. When you ring a bell, it is a symbolic marriage of the two polarities, the light and the dark. It goes to reason that a bell could be used in either manner.

Bells have been credited with judging one's deeds and rebounding those actions upon the ringer. Old lore speaks of placing a bell in a person's hands to divine any crimes. The bell was considered so pure that it would tap into the person's conscience and begin to hum if the individual was guilty of anything. Certain bells worn on the body served the purpose of magnifying the wearer's deeds, good or bad. In other words, if you rang a certain type of bell, it would read your soul and rebound what it found back onto you. If it judged you guilty of a crime, it would begin to hum on its own.

Bells are thought to mark time, protect, clear an area of vibrations, aid in creating a shift in consciousness, influence the weather, heal, aid in fertility matters, attract good luck, and relieve stress. In many traditions, bells are ritually consecrated or baptized before use.

Historically, to make use of the healing attributes of a bell, one would drink from it. This was said to cure stuttering and many other ailments.

Bells used for magical purposes should be metal. When metal strikes upon metal, it is a significant catalyst with a unique vibration. It is that vibration that is in harmony with magic and the universe. The vibrations of a bell are so strong that the ringing can take place underwater and still be heard on land. Legends state that in England, there are several drowned villages whose church bells can still be heard striking the hours from substantial depths.

A few bells have historically been assigned the duty of raising the dead or facilitating communication with them directly. These necromantic bells have a darker character than most bells and are ritually created to serve this specific purpose. Often, they feature engravings of words of power, along with the creator's name and birthday. The ceremony surrounding the creation of these types of bells is elaborate. They must be specially cast of seven metals and symbolically buried for seven days before they can be used.

Wind chimes were developed most extensively in Asia. Many consider these objects sacred, as they are thought to increase prosperity and promote well-being. They are hung both inside and outside of the home in an effort to smooth the flow of living energy. They promote peace, harmony, and tranquility.

According to the rules of feng shui, wind chimes have very specific requirements concerning rod count, base material, and which direction is best suited for hanging them. For example, if you wanted to reduce bad luck, you would use a five-rod metal wind chime and place it inside the home, never outside.

Bells and wind chimes create enchanting music, and music as a whole belongs to the realm of air. Throughout history, tales have been repeated extolling the virtues of music and its ability to affect the emotions, the conscious mind, and the subconscious. The Pied Piper enchanted children, Orpheus called wild beasts to sit calmly at his feet, the Sirens bewitched sailors, and snakes are charmed to this day by the vibrations that music produces. These magical vibrations bridge the communication gaps between humans and the rest of the universe.

Birds, Bees, and Butterflies

Bees are thought to be harbingers of good luck, for the most part. Spotting a swarm of bees in a garden is thought to indicate that prosperity is on the way. However, observing a swarm of bees surrounding a dead tree or hedge is a warning of death. Carrying a beehive over running water is thought to kill the bees.

Never swear in front of bees—they are of such noble character that it offends them. Honeybees were thought to be the tears of Re, the Egyptian sun god. They were also considered sacred to Artemis. Alexander the Great was embalmed in a coffin of honey because the substance is so pure.

Butterflies are thought to bring good luck. In many cultures, a butterfly is considered to be the soul of a recently passed human. Swarms of butterflies are thought to indicate that cold weather is on the way, as is having a yellow butterfly fly about the face.

Native American legends state that to have a wish come true, one need only whisper it to a butterfly, as they are the messengers of the Great Spirit. Fairies are known to ride on the backs of butterflies.

The most notorious bird, according to maritime folklore, is the albatross. Once believed to be the souls of drowned sailors, albatrosses were credited as being portents of furious storms and plagues of bad luck.

Blackbirds, which are sacred to the Celtic goddess Rhiannon, are thought to be the carriers of messages from the dead as well as portents of impending death. The crow has even more sinister attributes. A warning of impending disaster, the crow has been known to peck on windowpanes and alight on rooftops in order to gain the attention needed to spread its message. Moreover, crows warn of an oncoming famine when they flee as a group and warn of war if they fight in midair. A form of crow divination originated in ancient China.

The dove is associated with purity and inner light. It symbolically represents love. It is considered very bad taste to kill a dove and will bring bad luck upon the perpetrator. Long ago, it was believed that a person could not die if he or she rested on the feathers of a dove. Hence, dove feather pillows were used in hospitals and sick beds in an attempt to thwart death.

The eagle has always been linked with strength, regality, and immortality. The ancient Egyptians believed the human soul took on the form of an eagle after death. The shrieks of the eagle are thought to warn of death unless there are two or more, and then it is a call to bestow peace upon the land.

The heron is universally thought of as an omen of bad luck and impending disaster if it flies into a house. However, a hen is purposely carried into the home of newlywed couples in order to ensure prosperity and blessings.

The melodious lark is prized for its beautiful song, though it is considered bad luck to point at one. It is believed that if you point at a lark, a pus-filled sore will appear on the end of your finger.

According to Apache legends, hummingbirds have a special relationship with the wind. A young warrior known as Wind Dancer died while on an errand of mercy. His beautiful wife, Bright Rain, locked herself in her house out of grief. The wind brought a furious, cold winter. One day Bright Rain decided to take a walk. As soon as she stepped outside of her home, the weather turned beautiful again. Wind Dancer appeared to her as a hummingbird and stayed with her.

The hummingbird is considered a portent of rain and a blessing.

Sylphs and Fairy Folk

Sylphs are the nature spirits that inhabit air. They weave together the fabric of thoughts, dreams, communication, breathing, destruction, and secrets. Thought to be offspring of the Sidhe, sylphs are small in stature, transparent, and winged, and they move very quickly. Sylphs sometimes take on the form of birds, and other times clouds. At one time they were believed to favor virgins with their kinship. It is thought that sylphs control the winds and weather.

The Banshee is a member of the fairy realm that particularly relates to air. Described as a wailing shrouded figure with red eyes, the Banshee is thought to warn of impending death. Considered by some to be an aspect of the Morrigan, the Banshee is seen as a withered old crone with unkempt gray hair.

Italian folklore presents fairies that like to ride the noonday winds and steal kisses. Similar fairies appear as grasshoppers or as short gentlemen and women who are well dressed. Wind spirits are known to be playful and mischievous.

Modern society views almost all fairies as being of an airborne nature. Tinkerbell, the Disney character, is a manifestation of that view. Magic transports itself primarily through the vehicle of air, although in an etheric form, so the correspondence between the two is reasonable, if a bit misguided.

Weather and Sky

Humankind has used animals for ages as weather gauges, assigning certain behaviors to weather-related phenomena. Many of these old tales hold true and are eerily accurate. For example, a spider spins its web tighter if high winds or rains are expected. But if the web is weaved in the early morning hours, one can expect fair weather.

It is said that if a dog eats grass, one can expect severe weather, usually tornadoes or violent thunderstorms. Likewise, if the clouds and sky turn green, yellow, or black, a tornado is expected. Many types of bird calls are considered signals of oncoming rain. The same is true of increased activity levels among insects.

When doors and drawers stick, expect rain. Knots become tighter before rain. The sun and moon also help predict rain. Two old rhymes state that when either is reddish in color, rain will soon fall.

Over the course of history, strange things have fallen from, and been seen in, the sky. Fire, stones, sulphur, and even money have been known to fall from the sky. The simplest explanation for this is that over the course of a storm, all manner of things can be picked up and carried away by strong winds and later dropped. But sometimes these items manage to stay missing for years before they fall back to the Earth. Adding to this mystery is the fact that sometimes they fall from a clear, cloudless sky.

Thunderstones, according to Norse mythology, were missiles hurled by Thor to the ground as weapons against trolls. They were also used to protect against lightning. They actually were small pieces of quartz and other pebbles that appeared in freshly plowed fields. Thunderstones today are defined as ax-shaped stones that fall from the sky and have been scientifically proven not to come from a meteor source. Scientists currently have no explanation of how these objects manifest and fall into our planetary sphere.

Odd cloud shapes have inspired humankind for ages, and there is even a system of divination based on them. Similar to reading tea leaves, you first ascertain a primary shape from a cloud and then figure out how to apply that to your daily life lesson. People have envisioned the clouds as personifications of angels, spirits, and the breath of the Great Spirit itself. Clouds have been known to follow people, disappear by virtue of simply dissolving before one's eyes, and take on some very interesting shapes. They serve the purpose of keeping things hidden, forming a wall between the universe and the Earth. At the same time that they shield the lands from the sun's burning rays, they also serve as the mysterious veil that separates the planes of existence. It has been claimed that they serve as camouflage for alien life forms as well.

One of the strangest tales of anomalous clouds dates as recently as 1975. It relates that a young man had a cloud "purse its lips" and shoot a stream of water on him before disappearing. One can't help but wonder whom the young man had annoyed and laugh a bit. The Egyptian goddess Tefnut has been described in one of her depictions as a pair of spitting lips. Apparently, she has a great sense of humor as well.

Ghosts

Ghosts inspire both fear and fascination. Most often, ghosts are thought to be the souls of deceased persons. It is commonly believed that ghosts return to our plane because they have unfinished business. That business may be to seek retribution or simply to impart a message, but it is an almost universally accepted notion that they do have a purpose here.

Modern ghost hunters make use of high-tech gadgets to try to record atmospheric changes, magnetic polarities, and other environmental circumstances to help gain insight into what ghosts really are.

Ghosts can be both conjured and banished, but not with any guarantee. A banishing ceremony may work or it may not—it is up to that particular ghost. Free will carries over, to a large extent, and we can never be sure of intentions and circumstances outside of our own personal universe.

Some ghosts are energy imprints. When enough passion, life energy, and tragedy combine, it can have the effect of displacing time. The scene that encapsulated all of these emotions in such powerful forms repeats itself over and over, like a stuck record. The Hawaiian Night Marchers are ghost warriors that are considered to be both a projection of this life energy and passion and an imprint at the same time.

Other ghosts are a bit more interactive. They may be seen as shadowy figures or vapors, or they may look exactly like people. Some of them are quite belligerent or playful in their behavior, while others offer mere glimpses or aromas. Ghosts can easily drain a person's energy, so protect yourself by wearing silver or obsidian or carrying salt in your pocket.

One of the most frightening visages both of modern and ancient societies is the Old Hag. It is not known if she is a type of ghost or if she belongs to the fairy realm, but there is little doubt that she is a member of the Otherworld. Many legends speak of her waking those who are sleeping by choking them or riding their chests. Moreover, it is thought that she brings nightmares with her. For specific protection against the Old Hag, place in a small pouch a chunk of citrine, a chunk of jet, and healthy pinches of thyme, lemon balm, and passion flower. Sleep with this pouch hanging from your bedpost or placed under your pillow.

Dragons and Serpents

The ancient Aztecs depicted the element of air as a large feathered serpent who would "swim" across the skies. He was known as the god Quetzalcoatl. Curiously enough, such air creatures are found in many mythologies. The Japanese have a similar creature, without the feathers, in the Oriental dragon. Other beings of this sort are the rainbow snake (African) and the world snake (Egyptian).

Humans have documented sightings of these creatures since the year 793. The last recorded encounter with a sky serpent was as recent as November 29, 1883, in Maryland, and was witnessed by multiple people.

Sky serpents/dragons have shown themselves all over the world. In India, the primary home of colored rains, there is said to be a sky dragon whose urine will rot the skin of all it touches. Sky serpents are said to cluster around frankincense trees due to the pleasing aroma.

In China, sky dragons are seen as benevolent, wise, and protective creatures. They live for thousands of years.

AIR MAGIC

Air magic pertains to all things that travel through the air. This includes death, music, thoughts, spirits, dreams, and invisibility. Other specialty areas include travel magic and twilight studies. The word twilight is used here to describe the state of mind when we are not quite asleep and not quite awake. It is a shift in consciousness that allows for the more surreal parts of life to come into sharper focus.

Like dirt and water, each type of wind contains its own primary properties. The magical properties and purposes corresponding to the different types of winds are as follows:

Whirlwind: Whirlwinds run the gamut from gentle "dust devils" to full-blown tornadoes. This is a powerful aspect of wind to use; however, it is best to only use the violent form on the astral plane. This is the best wind to use to banish or destroy. Be careful with whirlwinds, even if only on the astral plane, because they tend to confuse.

South wind: The south wind is the warm wind of fire. It can work as an all-purpose magical booster; however, it can easily cloud a situation. The south wind brings blessings of friendship.

Singing into the south wind can facilitate contact with loved ones. It is the wind of celebration.

North wind: The north wind is the proverbial wind of change. It is the icy cold wind of death and works well in spells of destruction or banishment. It is connected to the element of earth and can be used as a healing wind. The north wind moves things forward in time.

East wind: The east wind relates to air. It symbolizes new beginnings and fresh starts. This is a good wind to use for matters involving intellect and self-improvement. It ushers in clarity and clears the mind.

West wind: The west wind is the wind of love and emotion. It relates to the element of water. Cleansing and divination are favored when the west wind is blowing. The voices of the dead are heard on the west wind.

AROMA MAGIC

Aromas can make us hungry or feel comfort and warmth, or inspire the opposite reactions. The power of scent works with the memory and the magical properties of the material. Incense, oils, herbs—all of these can be gently heated, burned, or used as is to inspire a bit of the sacred each time we breathe in. Aroma is a person's earliest sense. As babies, long before our eyes focus, we know our world from the scents that surround us.

Aromatherapy and flower essences, such as the Bach flower remedies, employ scent and vibrational energy in a therapeutic sense and have been proven to change one's mood. They can work both on the self and on others.

In order to use the essential oils listed here, simply dab the oil on a cotton ball and sniff, or place a few drops in an oil burner and gently warm the oil.

To boost memory: Rosemary

To inspire lust: Ginger or hibiscus

To decrease lust: Camphor

To inspire hunger: Cinnamon or garlic

To create an atmosphere of comfort: Cedar

To heal: Eucalyptus

To protect: Garlic

To revive energy: Peppermint

To create sacred space: Frankincense and myrrh

To attract money: Clove

To promote sleep: Lavender

To promote laughter and joy: Orange and lemon

To ease grief: Rose

To calm stress: Chamomile

To conquer fear: Grapefruit

To calm anger: Patchouli

AURAS

An aura is the colored area around the body. It is the atmosphere or spiritual essence of the self. It has been asserted that we each have a primary aura color. We cannot change our primary aura color, no matter what we do. However, there is an overlay of color on the aura that we can control and manipulate for magical use. This kind of magic should be used only on the self, never on others.

In order to manipulate your aura overlay, you have to be able to manipulate your emotions. In the same way that the mind "colors" emotion, the body reacts to the colors in the aura field. In other words, in order to change your aura overlay to a clear, bright red (to warn others away), you would need to direct the emotion you see as red into your projected aura. This is accomplished with concentration and visualization. If you can visualize something as simple as a bubble, you can change your aura overlay.

Here are the most commonly accepted aura color interpretations:

Red: Passion, sexual energy, anger

Orange: Stability, clear thinking

Yellow: Logic, intelligence, energy, nervousness

Green: Nature lover, healer, jealousy

Blue: Peace, at rest, depressed

Purple: Spiritual

Pink: In love

Black: Negative person

White: Connected to the divine, wise, a teacher of spirituality

In effect, manipulating the aura is akin to throwing a glamour. The difference is in the level of concentration. A glamour only has to be strong enough to fool an onlooker, while an aura manipulation has to fool you. If you are about to go into a job interview and are nervous, your aura overlay will be yellow. You might want to change it to an orange color, which indicates a clear thinking, stable person. So, you visualize the energy inside of you as a clear bright orange, then release it from the center of the self, allowing it to stream out of your pores into your aura field. Do not ground until after the interview. Have faith that your aura overlay is now orange, and it will be.

It is a smart move to make regular aura cleansings a part of your magical routine. The techniques are simple. While in meditation or as a separate task, simply visualize flooding your aura with a brilliant white light. Alternatively, you may want to smudge the aura field. Simply burn white sage or another cleansing herb in a dish, and direct the smoke all about your body with a feather or fan. Both techniques are safe and effective.

FEATHER AND FAN MAGIC

Feathers have symbolic links to deities and to the element of air. They have a living energy within them. It's always better to use found feathers than to buy them, if possible, because you can't be sure that the bird wasn't harmed unless it was a natural shedding process. The magical properties of feathers are as follows:

Blue jay: The feathers of a blue jay work well in happiness and emotional spells. They are commonly used to dispel depression.

Crow: The feathers of a crow work well in banishings and bindings. The feather of any black bird (except the black swan) will fill this role.

Hummingbird: Feathers from a hummingbird impart energy.

Kingfisher: The feathers of a kingfisher assure good fortune.

Owl: Owl feathers impart wisdom.

Peacock: Peacock feathers are sacred to the Orisha Ochun. They are protective and work well in beauty spells.

Robin: Robin feathers work well in wish magic, but you only get one wish per feather.

Sparrow: Sparrow feathers work well in healing spells.

Swan: Swan feathers are purifying and promote change. White swan feathers attract energy, whereas the black ones remove energy.

Turkey: These feathers are protective. A turkey feather makes the perfect quill pen for magical use.

Feathers are used in magic in many ways. They are placed in charm bags, worn, carried, made into dream catchers, and used to fan sacred smoke around an area and to direct energy. Feather fans are sacred. They decorate Orisha altars and make for good feng shui when hung indoors. You need not empower feather fans, as they have a natural energy of their own.

SMUDGING CEREMONIES

Smudging involves burning herbs and using the herbal smoke to cleanse and bless areas or people. It is a common and sacred practice.

Native Americans make use of three primary herbs for smudging: white sage, cedar, and sweet grass. The sage removes negative influences, the cedar cleanses the area, and the sweet grass calls in positive influences. The prayers said during the ceremony are lifted to the gods upon the smoke.

To smudge, place sand or salt in the bottom of a fireproof dish. If you are using a smudging wand, you can carry this dish beneath it to catch any hot ashes. If you are using a dried, crumbled herbal mixture, light a charcoal tablet and place it in the center of the bed of sand. Sprinkle the herbs over the charcoal as you move clockwise from area to area.

As you move around the space wafting the smoke, say aloud, "Only love and light may dwell here. All other vibrations must leave this house (person, etc.)." You may direct the smoke into corners and crevices with a feather, a fan, your breath, or your hand. When you have smudged the whole area, sweep the negative vibrations out the door and call in the positive vibrations that you want. Try something along the lines of, "Be gone, worry, pain, misery, and strife! Welcome, healing, comfort, love, and light!"

BALLOON MAGIC

I have used this simple technique a dozen or more times, and it always works. The latex in balloons does not biodegrade, so use of this technique is a personal choice.

To Banish

> 1 black balloon
> A small slip of paper
> A writing instrument

Write your banishing goal on the paper and slip it inside the balloon. Blow the balloon full while visualizing the object of your banishment leaving you and going inside the balloon. Tie the balloon shut. Say, "With sacred breath, I lay this problem to rest. Shall it now and forever go to sleep. Never to return, it ceases to be. The air has performed a clean sweep." Allow the wind to carry the balloon away, or let the balloon deflate on its own.

To Wish

> 1 balloon, color-coordinated to your personal set of correspondences
>   for your intent (for example, pink for love)
> A small slip of paper
> A writing instrument

Using the same simple technique as in the previous banishing spell, insert your written wish into the balloon. Say, "Heart's desire, by air and fire, I call you in these element's name! Come to me, my wish granted shall be, by the power of wind and of flame!"

SACRED RATTLES

Rattles are used both to summon and to disperse spirits. They are also considered protective and were historically used in this capacity as baby rattles. To make a basic gourd rattle, you will need the following items:

> A dry gourd at least 5 inches in diameter
> A handful of dried beans (to disperse) or dried corn (to summon)
> A stick for the handle of the rattle
> A peg to form a locking mechanism

Cut off the neck of the gourd. You may have to use a small handsaw to accomplish this. On the opposite end of the gourd, drill a small hole. Shake out all of the gourd seeds, saving them for later. Take a piece of heavy wire and stick it through the neck end of the gourd. Use this wire to scrape the pulp loose and then shake it out. Place your beans or corn inside the gourd cavity along with a few of the gourd seeds (about a dozen). To fashion the stick into a handle, whittle down the end of it so that it will fit into the gourd. It should be a snug fit, with a small amount sticking out of the top end. The protruding handle part should fit comfortably in your hand. At the tip of the rattle, where a small amount of the stick is protruding, drill a small hole into the stick and insert a peg to lock the rattle together. Now, the rattle is ready to decorate.

Alternatively, you may choose to cut the gourd in half, scoop out the pulp, decorate the gourd, and hot-glue it back together. You can carve or paint the surface or simply add beadwork and feathers.

Rattles can be shaken over items used in spell work to encourage change, or over one's body to remove negativity and speed healing.

FLYING OINTMENTS

Flying ointments traditionally are lard-based herbal blends that are smeared on the body to produce a vision of flying. Many of the ingredients that were used in the past were poisonous, such as datura and hemlock.

Flying ointments don't really cause Witches to fly through the air with their earthly bodies. Rather, they produce a psychedelic journey that takes place only in the mind and on the astral plane. It is a hallucination.

Flying ointments are linked to shamanic practices the world over. They are thought to increase one's awareness of the spiritual realm and bring one closer to God by facilitating an open channel. As the use of a true flying ointment is basically drug use, it is an individual choice. However, there are safer formulas that work with magic to promote these same types of journeys.

Flying Ointment

    Pure cocoa butter (you can buy this in stick form)
    Pinch of mugwort
    Pinch of bay leaves
    Pinch of parsley
    Pinch of tiny moonstone chips

Melt the cocoa butter and add the rest of the ingredients. Pour into a container and let cool. Empower the concoction with positive energy. When cooled completely, anoint the hands, feet, and pulse points.

INVISIBILITY

The power of the air is a tangible thing, yet it remains unseen. While no spell can actually render a physical body invisible, it can decrease a person's energy field, thereby making the individual less conspicuous. Magical cloaks have been accredited with this property for ages. Long ago, it was believed that digging up a dead body and switching clothing with it would render one invisible.

The most basic of techniques can be used to achieve a lower level of energy output, as described here.

Invisibility Spell

A piece of paper
A pencil

To begin, draw on the paper a picture of yourself or a symbol that represents you. When satisfied with the drawing, breathe on the paper to merge your essence with it. Enchant the paper by saying something along the lines of, "Glowing with life as I may be, I wish not for the world to see. My energy lies complete within me, as I speak it so mote it be!" Lightly erase the lines, leaving only the barest hint of an image on the paper. When you wish to end the spell, burn the paper while saying, "Back to full glow, my energy goes. Radiant with light, I return to sight!"

You can also make an invisibility powder by grinding fern, chicory, and poppy into a fine powder with a mortar and pestle.

DREAM MAGIC

Dream catchers, pillows, and journals are popular items for the Witch. Dreams open a world to us that is beyond our normal realm of perception. Stones and herbs can add vividness to our dreams. The extra boost of energy they impart allows us to remember our dreams more clearly. We can interpret the signs and symbols in our dreams to help us relate more effectively to the people in our everyday lives.

Dreaming takes place on the astral plane. It occupies the same space as magic. Dreams are the vehicle for departed souls and the gods to reach us and impart their messages.

Peaceful Dream Sachet

1 square of linen cloth
Piece of string
Lavender
Rosemary
Mugwort
Lemon balm

Take equal parts of each herb and tie them into the square of linen. Place the sachet under your pillowcase to allow the fragrance to drift about your head while at rest.

Blessing Your Dream Journal

Consecrate your dream journal to the elements. Inscribe inside it any personal symbols you wish and also this short incantation:

I will that this book serve to harmonize my spirit and mind.
May my spirit flow freely through the pages.
I shall discover myself here.
I will find my balance and healing.
I will experience joy and laughter.
May love and light surround me.
Blessed are the journeys.
Blessed is this book.
Blessed am I.
By babbling brook,
By flame and soil,
By breath and soul,
The dreams I have
Are remembered whole.
So mote it be!

You may anoint the journal with rosemary oil.

Dreaming Oil

> Rosemary
> Bay leaves
> 4 drops spearmint extract
> Almond base oil
> 3 marigold petals
> A few moonstone chips

Crush together equal amounts of rosemary and bay leaves. Add four drops of spearmint extract and blend into an almond base oil. Add three marigold petals and a few moonstone chips. Allow the oil to settle for thirty days in a dark place before use. Anoint pulse points or pillow. This oil promotes dreaming and helps you remember your dreams.

Dream Enhancers

Here are some other things you can do give your dreams a boost of energy:

1. Keep a moonstone or amethyst by your bed.

2. Make use of a dream catcher.

3. Record your dreams daily in your journal.

4. Keep track of what you eat for dinner the night before and which herb was prevalent in the meal.

5. Take a magical dream bath before retiring for the night. Passion flower or lavender scents work very well for this purpose.

6. Avoid taking medicines before bed.

OUIJA

Granted, the other elemental magic chapters did not really go into detail about the preferred divination systems, but Ouija belongs to an entirely different realm of magic. It is a simple form of necromancy, a form that requires the practitioner to be of a certain mindset to use it successfully. It does not work with one's natural intuition the way that other divination methods do. In fact, I would not call Ouija divinatory exactly, as it does rely on other forces for its ability to speak to us. Ouija is very tricky, because we cannot know for sure who is speaking to us. A skeptical mind is very important—as is respect.

Another school of thought teaches that Ouija *is* a divinatory device that taps into the deepest recesses of the human psyche to divine the answers to one's questions. People who believe this seem to have no trouble controlling the Ouija, but to me they are missing the whole point. Ouija is not a device designed to facilitate communication with yourself or your intuition; it is a device used to talk to the other side—those who have crossed over. I firmly believe that those who subscribe to this other school of thought are only fooling themselves about the purpose of Ouija. However, even if it is our intuition moving the planchette, Ouija would still be considered valid for the purposes of enlightenment.

The prejudice against Ouija in today's supposedly enlightened times is frightening. Even long-time Witches are known to associate it with uncontrollable forces and negative vibrations. They are missing a simple point. They are forgetting that they are in control of the whole session. Ouija facilitates contact only; it does not allow the spirit to conquer you or possess your soul—only you can do that. If you go into a session afraid, the Ouija will not disappoint you. If you go into it strong and confident, the experience could prove to be valuable.

These are the rules for successful Ouija use:

1. Always maintain control. Even if you are scared, remember that you can end the session at any time. If you do not know in your heart that you are in control, you won't be. It takes courage.

2. Never partake in Ouija without the proper wards in place. A sacred circle and protective incense are musts. A thorough cleansing afterward is also a necessity. If Ouija is so safe, why do I insist on this? Because it helps prepare your mind and boost your level of courage. And cleansing is just smart.

3. Always show respect to the spirit and insist on respect for yourself. Don't talk to spirits that only want to scare you or chas-

tise you. If you meet an unruly spirit, say, "Thank you very much. Goodbye." Then remove your hands from the planchette. Sometimes it takes several tries to reach a higher spirit. If you feel any negative vibrations, close contact. Likewise, if the spirit says goodbye rather quickly to you, respect that and let it go. Don't try to continue with questions that it does not want to answer.

4. Remember that spirits are the same in death as they were in life. You can come across those that are playing games, but you can also come across those that can help. Judge every session and spirit individually.

5. When you end a session, before you dismiss your circle it is wise to smudge the area. After circle dismissal, it is a good idea to smudge the whole house and yourself.

6. Keep a glass of water and a ruby or malachite stone close by at all times. If the ruby turns darker or the malachite develops a crack, end the session immediately, as this indicates an overabundance of negative energy. Keep a black candle burning to absorb and banish any negativity and a white one to attract and maintain purity. Empower the candles with these intents before use. *Important note:* These candles absolutely can *not* be used in any other sort of magical work. They can not be recycled, even if melted and repoured. When burned completely down, they should be buried in the ground—away from your property.

7. Keep your sessions short. Do not allow a session to continue for over thirty minutes at a time.

8. Never, ever use Ouija while under the influence of drugs or alcohol, not even cold medicine. Likewise, never use it when sick.

9. Do not carry out any requests that go against your ethics or better judgment. Never agree to do so in the first place. If you tell a spirit you will do something and then you don't follow

through, you are breaking a promise. This is not smart, and it allows the balance of control to shift.

10. Don't expect miracles. The Ouija will not give you winning lottery numbers or the location of buried treasure. Please hold more respect for this tool and the spirit on the other end of it than to try to use it for material gain. Ouija is a tool, not a game, no matter how it is marketed.

11. I've read many theories stating that one should never use Ouija alone. However, I have never had a problem with it. In fact, I prefer to use it alone rather than risk the possibility of allowing someone disrespectful to the spirits to communicate with them through my board. Use your best judgment. Keep the questions as simple as you can, and speak in a loud, clear voice.

Ouija Incense

This incense works best when powdered and burned on a charcoal tablet in a bed of salt. Combine equal amounts of lavender, cinnamon, and cedar with your mortar and pestle. Grind to a fine powder, using a deosil movement only. This formula will protect, continually keep the area clean, and facilitate harmonious communication. Watch the smoke carefully—sometimes a spirit will show its face in it.

AIR CORRESPONDENCES

Air is considered masculine and projective.

Season: Autumn

Magical virtue: To Know

Direction: East

Time of day: Dawn

Sense: Smell

Fluid: Saliva

Power animals: Eagles, ravens, hawks, sparrows, spiders, hummingbirds, monkeys

Places of power: Cliff tops, in the midst of a storm, anywhere with a clear view of the sky

Commonly associated colors: Yellow and silver

Linking items: Feathers, any type of smoke, fans, chimes, bells, flutes, kites, windmills, bubbles

AIR STONES

Amber: Amber serves the wind in a healing function. It is thought that wearing a necklace of amber will cure both asthma and whooping cough. It is a strengthening stone (technically it's a fossil resin) and is thought to be a lucky charm.

Aventurine: Aventurine helps in matters involving luck, peace, mental powers, and money.

Cat's-eye: The cat's-eye stone was once believed to aid in achieving invisibility. It is protective and a guardian stone.

Mica: Mica aids in protection and divination.

Pumice: Pumice is used to clean and beautify things. This stone floats on water. It helps in matters of protection and banishing. It can be used to absorb negative vibrations.

AIR HERBS

Agrimony: This herb is used in matters involving protection, sleep, and karma. Agrimony is known to reverse any hex and send it back to the sender.

Almond: Almonds aid in matters of wisdom and money.

Anise: Anise has been used for ages in matters of purification, protection, and restoring youth. It protects against nightmares. Anise also can call spirits to aid a person in magical work.

Bean: Dried beans are used in the making of gourd rattles used to disperse spirits. Beans are a protective and banishing substance. They also help bridge troubled waters and make way for peace in quarrels.

Benzoin: Benzoin is a preservative, but has its own magical properties too. It works well in purification rites and aids in attracting money.

Bergamot: Orange bergamot aids in money matters. Wild bergamot helps clarify situations.

Bittersweet: Bittersweet is protective and healing.

Borage: Borage strengthens intuition and courage.

Broom: Broom relates to the wind and has a large amount of lore connected to it. It is used for purification, calling rain, divination, calling wind, protection, sleep, and love attraction. An old legend states: Never sweep with broom in May, you'll sweep the head of the house away.

Caraway: Caraway protects against negative spirits and theft. The seeds are thought to attract love and fidelity as well as to strengthen the memory.

Chicory: Chicory helps curb free spending, removes obstacles, and helps achieve invisibility.

Dandelion: The dandelion is used for wish magic, divination, and calling spirits. Most often, the puffy seed head is blown and the results interpreted according to how many seeds are left.

Endive: A common salad ingredient and plate garnishment, endive can be used as an aphrodisiac. Make sure it is fresh—endive must never be over three days old.

Eyebright: Eyebright is used to strengthen intuition and clairvoyance.

Goldenrod: Goldenrod is used in matters involving money and divination and to find lost objects.

Gourd: Gourds are commonly used to make rattles that are then used to invoke or disperse spirits. They are protective.

Hazel: The wood of the hazel tree is used for making wands and crowns. Crowns made of hazel are said to help one achieve invisibility. Hazel nuts are used in matters of wisdom and fertility.

Lavender: Long used as a sleep aid, lavender also is an anti-nightmare charm when placed in dream pillows and the like. It induces feelings of happiness and peace. When carried, it is believed to aid one in achieving contact with the spirit world. It is used by Air Witches as protection when using the Ouija board.

Lemongrass: Lemongrass is planted around the home to protect and to repel snakes. It aids in intuitive matters and attracts love.

Lemon verbena: Long used in perfumes, lemon verbena is known for its love-attracting powers. It also works well in purification matters.

Lily of the valley: Lily of the valley is used to alleviate depression and attract happiness and peace. It also is thought to improve the memory. It is not advised to plant an entire bed of these flowers, however; legend states that to do so is to sign one's own death warrant.

Mace: Mace is burned or carried to improve the intellect.

Marjoram: Marjoram is used in matters involving protection, love, happiness, and health. It alleviates depression.

Meadowsweet: Another herb used to alleviate depression and instill peace and happiness, meadowsweet is also used to attract love.

Mint: Mint is healing, cleansing, and protective and inspires lust. It is specifically known to protect during travel. Mint is a good herb to use to cleanse an altar, as it dispels negative vibrations.

Mistletoe: Sacred to the ancient Druids, mistletoe has an impressive pedigree in magical matters. It is thought to protect from any sort of trouble. It exorcises negative vibrations, increases luck and fertility, and attracts love.

Mulberry: Mulberry is used in matters of protection and strength.

Parsley: Parsley promotes fertility and love. It has long been used as a plate garnishment due to its protective quality. It is used in purification rites.

Pine: Pine is protective and healing and attracts money. It is most often used in purification rites.

Pistachio: Pistachios have a curious history. They are thought to put zombies to rest and break love spells.

Rice: Rice is an important magical booster. When added to other ingredients, it is thought to increase the power of those items. It also is known to protect and increase luck on its own.

Sage: Sage is used for cleansing and purification, protection, wish magic, and healing. It is carried to improve the intellect.

Senna: Senna is a very useful cleansing herb and works well in matters of love.

Slippery elm: Slippery elm is known to stop harmful gossip in its tracks. It can also be used to instill eloquence.

Star anise: Star anise is used to boost magical power and promote good luck. It is commonly used as a pendulum. When strung and worn about the neck, it promotes intuition.

11

AIR GODS AND GODDESSES

THE JAPANESE WIND GODS

Japanese myths hold two major deities in charge of the wind. Shina-Tsu-Hiko is the god of the winds created by the breath of Izanagi. Shina-Tsu-Hime is the goddess of the winds and the wife of Shina-Tsu-Hiko.

The two were charged with filling the area between heaven and Earth and holding the Earth in place. They were worshipped for the most part by farmers and seafarers. The two Shinto gods are credited with the miraculous event of keeping away Genghis Khan's armies with severe winds in the thirteenth century.

Shinto, or the way of the gods, is Japan's original religion. The deities are called kami and are based on the forces of nature and life. It was said that when Shina-Tsu-Hiko was born, his breath was so potent that the mists lifted from the Earth, allowing the sun to shine for the first time.

There are other Shinto wind gods as well. Shina-To-Be, the couple's daughter, holds the special task of blowing away the mist or fog from the land. Tatsuta-Hiko along with Tatsuta-Hime blow fresh air into the fields to help produce rich harvests. Haya-Ji is the god of the whirlwinds. He is depicted as a horrifying, dark creature that carries the wind in a bag. Kami-kaze, which translates to "divine wind," is the god of storms and vicious cold wind. While each of these lesser gods is in charge of a specific type of wind, Shina-Tsu-Hiko maintains control over all of them.

Susanowo, the Japanese storm god, was well-known for being a young troublemaker. He was not content to rule only the oceans; he wanted the Earth and sky as well. The gods were repulsed by his behavior and threw him out of heaven. In his anger, Susanowo ripped out his fingernails and shaved his head bald. He came to Earth and made use of lightning and waves. He uprooted trees, destroyed buildings, and instigated all manner of chaos. His constant companion was Raiden, a monstrous thunder god depicted with red skin, claws, and horns. Raiden was the patron god of those who crafted the bow and arrows. He ruled over war and destruction. So violent were these two terrible gods that they once frightened the sun goddess, Amaterasu, into hiding. It took the dancing goddess of happiness, Uzume, to lure her back out into the sky.

LONO

Lono is the Hawaiian god of wind and storm. He also is the god of song, agriculture, sports, peace, learning, and fertility. It was thought that one was in the presence of Lono anytime one saw a storm, waterspout, or cloud or heard thunder or the sound of the wind. In fact, the greeting "Aloha" means "in the presence of wind, breath, or spirit." The Ti plant, also known as Ki, is sacred to Lono.

Lono was one of the original four gods that the people brought with them to Hawaii from Tahiti. It is said that he was the fourth to arrive. He was a shapeshifting god. In his human form, he was a light-skinned man, but it was more often that one would see him in his aspect of Kamapua'a, the pig-man. Kamapua'a was famed for his chaotic love affair with Pele, the Hawaiian volcano goddess.

Lono's Kamapua'a aspect was a thrill-seeking, tempestuous demigod of storms. He sought out the beautiful Pele, spurred on by the tales of her beauty. When he first lay eyes on her, he fell deeply in love and was consumed with passion. He approached Pele, who rebuffed him, saying, "You are but a pig." Kamapua'a took this as a challenge and invoked the rain. Pele laughed and said, "If you drown me, you will still not have me." She called upon fire to burn him. This soon became a pattern between the two, and the supreme gods worried the land would become so soaked that it would no longer be fertile or sustain fire. They commanded the two to stop. Pele yielded to Kamapua'a. They happily shared time together until their child was born. Then Pele went back to her philandering ways.

Lono ruled over four months of the year. During this time, no warfare was allowed; it was strictly a time of celebration. It was also during this time that rents and taxes were collected. This festival was called Makahiki. The chief was honored as a representative of Lono, and as such, offerings were gifted to him by the people. The chief would look over the offerings and then disperse them throughout the community, as was customary. During the Makahiki, it was taboo to do any work that was not necessary for survival. Makahiki contained many sporting events and dances. At the end of the festival, Lono was set adrift on his canoe, along with massive offerings, to wait until his return the next year at the ancestral land of Kahiki.

Legend also tells of how Lono came to Earth on a rainbow to marry Kaikilani, at which point she became the goddess Ka-iki-lani-ali'i-o-Puna. She and Lono lived together quite happily, enjoying their favorite activity of surfing. When an earthly being, a chief, attempted to seduce Kaikilani, Lono beat her to death. Kaikilani assured him, as he was beating her, that she loved only him and was innocent. His heart heavy with grief and sorrow, Lono went crazy for a time. He traveled the islands fighting every man he came across as an attempt to purge his heart of pain. Finally, he set sail alone, assuring all that he would return. Through these events, Lono created the festival of Makahiki, in honor of his dead wife.

Lono is representative of two distinct forms of nature: the spirit of the natural world, which is present all around us, and the spirit of our conscious mind. Lono is not only the spirit of nature, he is our spirit.

OYA

Oya, also known as Yansa, is the Orisha who rules the wind in Santerían traditions and Yoruban myths. She is both the soft, caressing breeze and the hurricane-force gale. Her name means "the tearer," as it was she who, when angered, would tear the leaves from the trees. She is the daughter of Yemaya, the Orisha of the sea. She is also the goddess of the rainbow.

Oya is depicted as a beautiful, strong, courageous woman. She is said to have long, dark hair and copper skin and is most often dressed in a skirt of nine colors. She wears a nine-pointed crown and nine copper bracelets. However, it is also said that her face is so terrible to look upon that it will cause instant insanity. In ceremonies where Oya is called down, no one looks directly at her. Her sacred color is a deep wine, her sacred number is nine, and her day is Wednesday. She is said to prefer flowers on her altar, and she holds sacred the cowrie shell, the monkey, and the buffalo. Traditionally offered foods are rice and black beans.

Oya represents the roots of both life and death, as she personifies sacred breath. She rules over all breathing problems and lapses in memory and has been known to use electrical currents to punish those deserving. It is not recommended that one attempt to brush her off; she is to be taken seriously and revered. Oya is said to have one fear, and only her husband, the Orisha Chango, knows what it is (although it has been speculated that it is the head of a ram). She is a warrior queen and thought to be quarrelsome. As the Orisha of the wind, she is turbulent and can be quite mad. She can be considered jealous and demanding. She does not like to be second-guessed or told what to do. She is fiercely independent.

Oya is known to be the spirit that guides the soul after death. She rules over cemeteries and is said to be most often found there. No other Orisha is thought to be brave enough to face death and guide the mortal soul after its passing. Yet, Oya is compassionate. Her legends recount many tales of sick children that she allowed to live as a gift to the parents.

It is said that when there is a tornado, it means that Oya is walking the Earth. When there is a hurricane, she is angry. It is Oya's task to create confusion, but from this confusion new opportunities are born. She incarnates the winds of change and blows away the past, making way for new beginnings.

In one legend, Oya saved her husband from certain death. The tale relates that Chango came to her house, being chased by his enemies. He asked Oya to help him bide his time so that he could rest and prepare for the battle. Oya dressed him in one of her dresses and cut off her hair, placing it on his scalp, to fool his enemies. Once Chango emerged from her abode, the battle was underway. Oya took her place by his side and fought valiantly. The trick worked, and Chango was saved.

In Brazil, Oya is called Iansa. In this area of the world, she rules over sexual pleasure. It is said that she asked to serve the male Orishas in a sexual capacity in return for them teaching her all about the world. When she met Chango, she fell madly in love, and he revealed to her the secrets of thunder and lightning.

According to African belief, all female Orishas are represented by rivers. They all are also considered to be Witches and hold the secrets to powerful magic.

Oya has an even darker side than that of tornadoes and fierce winds. She carries disease and madness on her breeze, specifically diseases of the skin. She rules over the realm of insanity.

Oya faced reproduction problems. One story relates that she had to use a magical charm from an anthill to become pregnant. Her husband, Chango, was then able to impregnate her, yet this was credited to the fact that he is a violent, and therefore virile, god. Chango ruled over storms until he was overthrown because of his cruelty.

YAPONCHA

Yaponcha is the Hopi wind god. He lives at the sunset crater (a volcano) in a crack of a black rock. One legend relates that he was a very troublesome god who always blew the seeds from the fields; hence, the crops failed to grow. The Hopi elders went to the "little people" for help. The two little people who accepted the task of stopping the wind were Po-okonghoya and his brother Palongahoya. Both were war gods. The two went to their grandmother, the Spider Woman, and asked her to make them a sweet cornmeal mush to carry with them on a journey.

After four days of traveling, they reached the rock. They took the mush and sealed up the crack. This made Yaponcha very angry.

As the days went on, the land became hotter and hotter. Finally, the elders went to the little people again, asking for relief from the heat. The two obliged and went back to the rock and opened a tiny hole. Yaponcha appeared as a tiny cloud, and the land cooled once more.

The blowholes in the volcanic surfaces were very important to the Hopi tribes. Quite often, the larger farms would be placed close to a blowhole, to assure rain.

Yaponcha is honored in the month of March. It is Yaponcha who is credited with leading the Hopi tribes to their sacred land. He blew them across a great lake.

THE FOUR WINDS

Within Witchcraft, the functions of the four winds are primary to any set of correspondences. The Greek cross is said to be a representation of the four winds, with one arm shooting out in each direction. It is now known that Native American tribes used this symbol in the same manner as the ancient Greeks.

The four winds span almost all mythologies. We find them in Greek, Roman, Celtic, Babylonian, Christian, and Native American legends and texts. Frequently, they are the compass points, or four directions. While there are adverse winds and crosswinds to contend with, some claim between eight and twelve total. For the purpose of this discussion, we will stick to the main four.

In the Greek myths, there are four separate deities in control of the winds, each with a specific direction and specific functions. The four deities are directly ruled by Aeolus, who is known as the king of the winds. Aeolus is said to be married to Eos, the Greek goddess of the dawn. The four winds are their children.

Odysseus visited Aeolus, who received him happily and gifted him with a bag containing any winds that would cause him to stray from his course, so he could return to Ithaca that much sooner. While Odysseus slept, his crew opened the bag, hoping it was filled with treasure. The winds escaped and blew Odysseus further off course.

The myths relate that Poseidon, the father of horses, is the grandfather of the winds. Several of the tales featuring Boreas and Zephyrus include this aspect, as the winds were seen as horses at times.

Boreas is the Greek god of the north wind. He is a stormy personality, known to be violent when irritated. The other gods were known to petition Boreas for help in aggravating mortals with whom they were displeased. Hera asked Boreas to help destroy Hercules, and Boreas was responsible for his shipwreck on the island of Cos. Boreas was known to provide sailors with enough wind to get them home as well.

Boreas is sometimes depicted as having twin serpent tails for feet. However, he is most often represented as having a gray beard, long, shaggy hair, a very muscular body, and amber wings and wearing a short tunic.

Boreas was not the type to be denied something he wanted. Such was the case with the woman he loved, Oreithyia. Boreas loved her and continually asked her parents for her hand in marriage. They kept delaying, which frustrated Boreas. It seems Boreas had a problem of which they did not approve: he simply could not breathe easy. When he would breathe, fierce winds would blow. Finally, fed up with the runaround, Boreas acted upon his true nature. Impatient to be with the woman he loved, he saw her at play in a field. He swooped down, carried her off, and ravished her. She became his wife and bore him twin sons, who were later killed by Hercules.

Oreithyia was the princess of Athens, so the city adopted Boreas as their brother-in-law and petitioned him for help during the battle of Artemisium. Boreas visited the enemy with a storm, which was so powerful that it sunk four hundred of their ships. The people were so grateful that they erected a sanctuary in his honor and celebrated the anniversary of the storm annually in a festival called Boreasmi. Boreas was the "winds of change" personified.

Zephyrus is the Greek god of the west wind. He is the gentle wind, most often seen as benevolent. It was his sacred duty to cool the fields at Elysium. He is usually depicted as young, handsome, and most often naked.

However, he was prone to jealousy. Zephyrus, like many of the Greek gods, was bisexual. He had fallen in love with a handsome youth named Hyacinthus. The two were happy together until Apollo seduced Hyacinthus. After that, Hyacinthus seemed to prefer the company of Apollo. One day while Apollo was teaching Hyacinthus how to throw a discus, Zephyrus, in his jealousy, blew the discus back upon Hyacinthus, striking him dead. Apollo was grief stricken. He wished that he could change places with Hyacinthus, but could not. So he turned him into a beautiful flower, the hyacinth.

Zephyrus fell in love with the goddess Chloris (known to the Romans as Flora) and gifted her with the dominion over all flowers. He married her, but only after he abducted and raped her. The two were thought to be happy together and had three children.

Zephyrus had an affair with the Harpy Podarge. The coupling produced Xanthus and Balius, the immortal horses of Archilles.

In Roman legends, when Psyche (the Greek goddess of breath) fell into disfavor with Venus, she retreated to a mountaintop. Due to her inability to attract a husband, despite her magnificent beauty, Psyche agreed to marry a monster. Zephyrus saw the beautiful maid standing there, alone and terrified. He gently picked her up and carried her to a flower-filled field. Exhausted, Psyche fell into a deep sleep.

When she awoke, her mind was calm and she could once again think. Upon exploring the area, she found a stunningly beautiful palace. She entered and looked around in delight at the amazing objects and artwork. She heard a voice telling her that this was her new home and to go to her chambers, where a supper would soon be sent. She did as she was told. As time passed, Psyche never laid eyes upon her new husband, but only heard his voice and felt his touches in the dark of the night. She was treated well, but longed to see his face. She called Zephyrus to her again and entreated him to take an invitation to her sisters.

The sisters visited, born in the arms of Zephyrus, and they were envious of Psyche's palatial home. Out of jealousy, they told her to hide a lantern and gaze upon her husband in his sleep. When Psyche followed their advice, Cupid left her, citing that love could not live where suspicion dwells.

Each of the sisters thought they would try to win Cupid's affection for themselves and climbed the steep mountain. They called upon Zephyrus to carry them to Cupid's home once again and jumped into his arms. However, Zephyrus did not catch them, and the sisters plunged to their deaths, one by one.

The Greek god of the south wind is Notus. He is depicted as a young man with long hair. The Greeks were afraid of Notus, because he was strong and dynamic. Notus was known to pair up with Boreas and create powerful storms.

Eurus is the Greek god of the east wind. He was seen as a curly-haired young man, with a beard and a look of sadness etched onto his face. It was Eurus who brought the strong rains and storms. He was seen as the unfavorable wind, yet he often showed kindness to humans.

The four winds represent much more than just winds—they represent the seasons of the year and the cardinal directions. Boreas is seen as winter, Notus as autumn, Zephyrus as spring, and Eurus as summer. While it may seem odd that the south wind corresponds to autumn and not summer, it is because that is when that wind is the most active, at least in Greece.

The wind gods are said to have an affinity for the scent of frankincense.

In ancient Greek society, violent storm winds were seen as monsters instead of gods. They were kept locked in a cave by King Aeolus and only released to do the bidding of the gods. Among them was the fierce Typheous, who was said to be the father of all monstrous winds.

Typheous was also the father of Ceberus, the three-headed dog who guarded the entrance to Hades.

Typheous was represented in many monstrous forms. He was shown as a fire-breathing dragon with one hundred heads and as a gigantic human to the waist with snakes for legs and fingers. He had dirty, unkempt hair and pointed ears, and his eyes flashed fire. Gaia had given birth to him in an attempt to prevent the overthrow of the Titans. Typheous was so fierce that it almost worked.

The word typhoon comes from the root word of Typheous, as he was known to create these violent storms as well as to hurl volcanic rock at those who displeased him. Typheous was known for his violent temperament and lawless ways. Taming him was not an option, so Zeus locked him away.

Homer relates that Typheous was born out of jealousy. Hera, consumed with bitterness because Zeus had birthed Athena without her, fell upon her knees and demanded from Gaia a child of her own. Gaia answered her with Typheous.

SHU

Shu is the Egyptian god of air. He is most often represented in human form, wearing a large feather on the top of his head. It was his task to fill the space between the heavens and Earth. He held in place the body of his daughter, Nut, the Egyptian sky goddess.

Shu's name translates to "he who rises up" and "emptiness." He is also thought to be the god of sunlight. He was wed to his twin sister, Tefnut, the Egyptian goddess of moisture. The two produced both Nut and Geb, the god of the Earth. In the oldest legends of Egyptian antiquity, it was Shu who brought Re into being.

Shu was said to dwell with Re in the heavens, while his wife identified with the moon. One of Shu's darker aspects is that of executioner, a death personification. In the Underworld, he rules a band of torturers and punishes the wicked.

When King Tutankhamun's tomb was opened, it was found to hold a headrest depicting Shu. He cradled the heads of the dead between two lions. Symbolically, this represents the sun resting between days and a faith in reincarnation. Shu was considered to uphold the sun in the same manner. It was his role to hold the sun in the sky.

Shu had more protective aspects too. As he was the sacred breath of life, it was Shu that brought about each new day. He is often represented as a lion.

ODIN

Odin is the father god of the Norse pantheon. He is most often depicted as an old man with one eye, a beard, and long gray hair. He was known to change shape according to his moods. Odin had two ravens as constant companions named Hugin and Munin ("thought" and "memory"). He commanded a pair of wolves named Geri and Freki.

Odin ruled the world from his palace named Valhalla. Valhalla was known to never run empty of mead, for Odin possessed a magical goat, Heidrun, that dispersed it through its udder. The Valkyries would serve it to the assembled warriors in preparation for the final battle. There was also a magical boar that would be cooked and served and then spring back to life, only to be cooked again. The theme was that one would never go without in Odin's palace, and only the finest warriors were taken there. These warriors were chosen by the Valkyries, who served Odin. In order to gain entrance, one had to die fighting.

Odin had sacrificed himself by hanging for nine days upon the Yggdrasil tree with a spear embedded in his side. He did so to gain the knowledge of magic and the runes. Odin was a constant seeker of knowledge. He gave up an eye to drink from the well of Mimir, which was known to impart great knowledge.

Odin was treacherous, a breaker of oaths. He would resort to whatever means necessary to accomplish his goals. An example of this is the method in which Odin laid claim to his famed eight-legged horse, Sleipnir. After the war between the old gods of nature, the Vanir, and the new gods, the Aesir, the walls surrounding Asgard (the kingdom) needed to be rebuilt. A tall man came across the rainbow bridge of Bifrost enquiring if he could perform the work. In exchange, he wanted the goddess Freya, the sun, and the moon. Odin was furious and ordered the man to leave Asgard at once. Clever Loki went to

Odin with a plan. He proposed that they give the man the work and a six-month time limit in which it must be completed. There was no way the man could do that, and it would save the gods some work, as the wall would be partially built. Odin decided to implement Loki's plan. The man agreed to the terms if he would be allowed to use his horse for help. The gods saw no harm in that and allowed him to do so.

The work commenced at a furious pace. All winter long, the man and his horse worked tirelessly, hauling loads so heavy that they held the gods themselves in wonder. The gods quickly realized that there was something sneaky going on. They all turned on Loki and started screaming, because it was all his idea. Three days before the work was completed, the horse broke free from his rein and chased a beautiful mare into the field. The man gave chase, but it was of no use. He continued the work the next day on his own, barely accomplishing anything. When the sun rose and set and turned the season to summer, the man had lost the bargain. He stormed into the palace raging, and Thor struck him on the head with his mighty hammer. Thor had realized over the course of the work that it was no man, but a giant in disguise.

A few months later, Loki came home leading the escaped horse and the young colt Sleipnir. Odin claimed Sleipnir as his own. In order to save Freya, Loki had shapeshifted into the beautiful mare that had led the horse away. The colt Sleipnir was produced from a union between Loki and the swift horse.

Odin required human sacrifice and preferred to be worshipped by warriors and noblemen. The most common method of sacrifice was to hang the victim, impale him on a spear, and set him on fire. Odin's favor was heavily courted, because he was the god who presided over victory and war. He could easily turn a losing situation into a winning one. The only question was, would he? He was well-known as a betrayer of warriors. It was Odin's goal to get as many warriors as possible to Valhalla before the final battle began. Worshippers could make offerings and sacrifices to him and fight for him, but this did not guarantee that their lives would be spared. He could give them victory, but would not. To do so would defeat his own goal. Odin's goal was to win the final battle so that the world he created could continue—to do otherwise would mean its demise.

Odin was a wanderer. He roamed the world with a giant staff and was often kept company by Loki, his blood brother. Loki is said by some to be a dark aspect of Odin.

Odin ruled the Berserkers. The Berserkers would fight in such a state of fury that they could continue fighting even when mortally wounded. They were known to partake of all manner of drug and drink in excess. They often reached a point in their rage and drug-induced madness where they could not tell enemy from friend and would simply kill whichever one happened to be there. They would call upon the spirits of bears to possess them and impart courage and ferociousness. While they were fierce warriors, they were despised for their unforgivable cruelties and eventually were outlawed.

PART FOUR
FIRE

12

THE PATH OF THE FIRE WITCH

The path of the Fire Witch is not for the faint of heart. Strong and courageous, these Witches rarely take no for an answer. The Fire Witches are considered to be the rebels of the Elemental Witches. They possess a joy of life that is unequaled. They are extremely sociable creatures.

The Fire Witches are all about individuality. Each one is unique. For the most part, their lives are beautiful and poetic, yet there lurks an underlying current of tragedy. There is no typical personal style to the Fire Witch; it varies, as does each flame. The one thing you can be sure of is that she will shine. In blue jeans or diamonds, you know a Fire Witch by the confident aura that surrounds her.

The Fire Witch's decorating style runs the gamut from sleek, modern, and sophisticated to all-out opulence and luxury. She has a flair for decorating, often incorporating candles and designer lighting to add a more dramatic touch. Frequently, Fire Witches love antiques and metal objects. Their homes often feature warm, rich colors and dark woods.

The Fire Witch's home is usually very neat and clean. She will spend whatever time is necessary to keep it that way. She will also destroy that cleanliness in an instant, when she is angered enough, by having a complete and total hissy fit, although that is rare. While the Fire Witch can be hotheaded and temperamental, her iron will usually allows her to maintain control.

The Fire Witch is often a gourmet cook, with a taste for the finer things in life. She is all about quality over quantity. However, this love of good food can manifest in two ways: she may carry a few extra pounds, or she may be too thin. A predisposition for both anorexia and obesity is within the element of fire; hence the Fire Witch must be careful in all weight issues.

The Fire Witch loves to dance and is very seductive, passionate, and lusty. She can be indulgent when it comes to her sexual nature. She often is very active and usually loves to participate in sporting events. She is bold and daring and frequently pushes things to the absolute limit.

Because of her indulgent habits, the Fire Witch may unknowingly enable addictions or foster one of her own. Some Fire Witches may have addictive personalities. When a Fire Witch loves someone, she does so with a heart so pure that she can overlook any defects in the person for a long time.

This can place her in troublesome relationships until she has finally had enough and moves on. When a Fire Witch moves on, she has a compulsion to completely destroy the previous bond and is capable of being cruel in order to see to it that the situation is over for good. She is much more comfortable knowing that it cannot be repaired and can move herself forward more easily by not allowing herself to wonder about the past.

Philosophically, the Fire Witch has an open mind. She is the proverbial free thinker. Because of the placement of her element (both above and below the Earth), the Fire Witch has the ability to see all sides of any argument. She values honesty and courage above all else. There is nothing she detests as much as a liar. Fire Witches are usually quick-witted, think-on-their-feet types of folks. There is a reason that smart people are called "bright."

The fire brings the light, and with light there follows shadow. The Fire Witch is complex, passionate, and tumultuous. She is sizzling hot stuff. She has both a light and a dark side, and the two sides work together constantly.

The light side of the Fire Witch keeps her personal practices of spirit informal and fun. But when it comes time for magical work, the shadow side often takes over. The dark side of the Fire Witch holds a vast knowledge of the more complex magical applications. Magical equations and ceremonial practices are second nature to the Fire Witch. She may prefer the drama of a high magic ritual and a more ordered structure to things. However, she often utilizes a simpler style of Witchcraft, too. It depends on the situation.

Magically, the Fire Witch specializes in bonding with divinity, regeneration, energy, truth, manifesting, sex magic, banishing, purification, destruction, negative magic, and defensive magic.

Fire has been used to honor the gods since its inception. Many shrines and altars are guarded by an eternal flame. The Fire Witch understands that her every movement is an honor to divine forces.

She is very generous with her time and money when it comes to charity. She always seeks to help and improve the world around her in this manner.

Fire is a creative element, especially when seen in its regenerative aspect. In the same manner that the phoenix rises from the ashes or the sun undergoes an eclipse, a Fire Witch puts herself through a constant process of growth by tearing herself down in order to build herself anew. It can be an agonizing process, but she emerges renewed and stronger than ever. She will often disappear from the world for a few days at a time due to this process. She can be instrumental in helping others move beyond their own heartbreaks and pains and begin their lives again.

Often, the Fire Witch will take painful experiences and channel them into some form of art. She may be especially talented at working artistically with metal, even if she does not know it yet.

The Fire Witch holds herself to an uncompromising code of honor and ethics. She will bestow justice and be benevolent at the same time.

She operates from a basic moral code of what is right and what is wrong and rarely will go against her gut instinct. Because of this, Fire Witches make excellent law enforcement officers. Due to their love of numbers, they fare well in the fields of science and computers. They often understand the numeric codes presented within dreams to be prophetic and can easily recognize patterns.

Friends of the Fire Witch are used to her stealing the spotlight—she knows how to get attention! She naturally projects a warm yet noble aura. If you don't want to hear the truth, don't ask a Fire Witch. She can be both gentle and blunt. The key is to hear her out. Fire Witches seem lit from within and glow with a special radiance.

Fire is purifying, and the Fire Witch tolerates no political agendas among her friends and family. If she spots a troublemaker or rumor-monger, she will quickly call the person on it.

Fire Witches can be extreme in their behaviors and emotions. They tend to see things in terms of black and white, due to their strong moral instincts. Yet, while Fire Witches can be rigid in certain areas, they are the most playful and joyous of the Elemental Witches. They seem to be always smiling, always willing to try something new. They push harder and climb higher—there are no limits for fire folk!

While water is creation, earth is rebirth, and air is death, fire is the divine spark of it all. No other Elemental Witch understands the process of regeneration the way the Fire Witch does. She truly grasps purification of the spirit. In the same way a medical doctor cauterizes a wound to stop the bleeding, the Fire Witch can cauterize the soul to stop emotional pain and make way for healing. She concentrates her life on matters of the spirit and advancement. She is talented in all areas related to working with the spirit and Otherworld spirits. She can call and banish spirits quite easily, but never does so wantonly. She has great respect for the other planes of existence.

Fire Witches are the explorers of the universe. Due to their role as spiritual connectors, Fire Witches can easily accomplish astral projection. (To learn more about the spiritual connector inherent in fire, see the section "The Eighth Chakra" later in this chapter.) The element of earth manifests itself in humanity as the body, air as sacred breath and mental faculties, and water as body fluid and emotions, but fire is the collective energy that animates the body. Fire represents the electrical impulses in the brain and body that make life possible.

Many cultures, no matter what their collective vision of the afterlife is, report that people who undergo near-death experiences first see a beautiful white light. When we work with chakras, we are working with light. All magical work that incorporates light and spiritual advancement falls in the realm of the element of fire.

The role of the Fire Witch is one of independence. She encourages people to stand up for themselves and will not hesitate to stand up for herself. Coming under fire by others does not scare her; it inspires her. She is most comfortable when she is free to express her opinion completely, and she usually detests censorship. The Fire Witch takes an active role in all areas of life. If something isn't working, she is the first one to work to try to change things for the better.

The altar of the Fire Witch usually contains various metals, such as brass, silver, iron, and copper. Likewise, it often holds several candles. Her power is at its peak during the summer months. Popular summertime activities like vacations, camping, swimming, and picnicking are borne of the inspiration of fire. Fire teaches us to enjoy the zest life has to offer. While a Fire Witch can be zealous in her career ambitions, she never forgets to enjoy her life. In the winter months, when the days are short, the Fire Witch undergoes a period of reflection that further defines her path. She is still there, doing everything she normally does, but her focus has turned inward to her home and family. It is a process of reaffirming relationships that takes place every year. Even the bright light of the Fire Witch can grow dim at this time, and depression can set in. Luckily, a few bites of a tropical fruit, a warm fire in the fireplace, and a few candles later, she's as good as new.

THE DARK SIDE OF THE FIRE WITCH

The vibrant Fire Witch has her dark side too. She can be pushy and very sarcastic. Stubborn to the bone, she does not deal well with disagreements. She fully realizes that no one can be right all the time, unless, of course, it's her. When angered, she may have a tendency to make fun of others. She can be quite arrogant and, as a result, is very hard to teach. The Fire Witch learns best when left to do her own thing. There is no substitute for life experience. At times, her sarcasm can manifest as a biting sense of humor, but at other times, it is disparaging and hurtful. She may have a bad habit of talking down to others and, instead of listening, prefers to play the devil's advocate. When doing so, signals can easily be crossed, and what she thinks is simply pointing out alternative options for others to consider, they may interpret as her telling them they are wrong, when that is often not the case at all.

FIRE WITCH LORE

The Aurora Borealis and Other Natural Lights

Also known as the northern lights, the aurora borealis is nature's primary light show. It is described as beautifully colored mists that weave and dance their way across the skies. These stunning lights are shared between fire and air, but are listed under fire because no light would exist if not for fire's eternal source.

The northern lights are actually a gathering of solar-charged particles attracted to the Earth's magnetic pull, but the Vikings believed the lights to be the spirits of dead maidens dancing. This belief crossed cultures, and the Native American tribes that lived in the extreme north also associated these lights with the realm of the dead. They believed that they could call these spirits forth by whistling.

In ancient times, some people were afraid of the lights. They saw them as ominous portents of war or famine. They thought that when the lights appeared, it meant the gods were angry.

Will-o'-the-wisps are the earthbound lights that guide travelers away from safety to walk along treacherous paths. They can be considered malevolent, and in the past were often thought to be the souls of the dead. They tend to appear on swampy lands and near graves.

Will-o'-the-wisps are most often described as floating orbs of light that can move about quickly. They have been reported in a wide range of colors. Many who experience the phenomenon say that the light mimics their movements and pace.

Currently explained as a glowing type of swamp gas, will-o'-the-wisps continue to make their presence known in various parts of the world. They are also called ghost lights, spook lights, corpse candles, foxfire, fairy lights, and peg-o'-lanterns (or jack-o'-lanterns).

In North Carolina, at Brown Mountain, these lights are particularly active. The first recorded encounter with these mysterious lights was in 1771, by a German engineer. Later accounts related that these lights would chase travelers along the trails. Of all of nature's eerie lights, the will-o'-the-wisps are the only ones credited with actually following people and having a seemingly coherent thought process.

In Irish folklore, the will-o'-the-wisps are described as being quiet and helpful. They appear in order to warn one of possible bad health for family members or loved ones.

While scientists say that will-o'-the-wisps are burning balls of swamp gas, they are known to be cold. They have also been reported to move against the wind, something a real gas cloud could not do.

They have also been called "ball lightning" and are said to explode and crackle with energy. Ball lightning has been credited with causing deaths. In 1638, ball lightning struck a church in Devon County in the United Kingdom, subsequently killing four people.

Often, ball lightning disappears as quickly as it appeared, leaving witnesses bewildered. Sometimes, an explosion is heard just after the light disappears.

St. Elmo's Fire, on the other hand, is seen as a benevolent force of nature that guides sailors through treacherous areas and signals the end of storms. It is said to be the dead spirit of St. Erasmus returning to aid the sailors. St. Elmo's Fire is actually a form of atmospheric electricity that appears during stormy weather.

Lightning

Lightning is a manifestation of fire in the air. Wielded by the gods as both a weapon and a messenger, lightning is nature's fireworks. It is our basis for electricity.

Folklore relates that lightning never strikes in the same place twice. However, this is simply untrue. The Empire State Building was struck no less than sixty-eight times in a three-year span. Park ranger Roy Sullivan from Waynesboro, Virginia, holds the world record for being struck by lightning more than any person in history. Between 1942 and 1983 he was struck an astounding seven times.

The ancient Romans thought that a lightning bolt striking from left to right was a sign of good fortune. If the bolt passed from right to left, it meant the gods were unhappy with current events.

It was believed that examining sites where lightning had struck would reveal lightning stones. Lightning stones are the small ax-shaped stones also called thunderstones and are thought to hold the magical properties of lightning. Temples were often erected on these sites, as they were considered sacred.

When lightning strikes, the air around it warms. Lightning is such a pure source of fire that it can heat the air to five times hotter than the surface of the sun. This causes the crackling thunder sounds, due to the rapid expansion of air forced by the heat.

In myths, the most powerful of the deities held the secret of lightning: Zeus in the Greek myths, Thor in the Norse myths, Chango in the Yoruban myths, and Pele in the Hawaiian myths.

In South Africa, anything that has been struck by lightning is considered taboo. A tree that has been struck may not be used for fire, animals may not be eaten (without the proper cleansing ceremonies), and so on. It is generally thought that anything selected by nature to be struck down by lightning would be unlucky to use, and possibly draw the lightning toward it.

Some South African tribes believe that if they dig where lightning has struck, and eat shavings of what is left in the ground by the lightning, they are consuming the power of the lightning bolt. Consuming the lightning bolt is most often reserved for the tribal "doctor" and gives him the ability to divert storms from the village.

In various parts of the world, lightning is thought to take on the physical form of a bird. In some places this lightning bird is called the "bird of heaven." It is described as iridescent.

If you see a flash of lightning, it is because the lightning bird has just darted across the sky. It is thought that if you destroy the nest of this bird, there will be a great storm. In general, taking any negative action against this bird is inviting misfortune. It is said that no person has ever succeeded in harming this bird, as it moves too quickly.

In order to protect a village from lightning, certain tribes believed that they had to dig up the eggs the lightning bird left behind. Anyplace that had been struck by lightning was a possible breeding ground. The thought was to destroy the eggs, but all too often they were left intact. The eggs of the lightning bird are thought to be valuable lucky charms.

Lightning is predominantly thought to be born only from the sky, but in actuality it is the combination of a positive charge from the ground surging upward and the negative charge of the lightning surging downward that creates the electrical charge of lightning. Lightning strikes both ways.

Often, when lightning strikes the ground, it will fuse the minerals underneath into a rock formation. So the eggs of the lightning bird and Chango's stones do indeed exist. The minerals present in the soil vary from region to region and determine the rock produced. When lightning strikes sand, it fuses the grains together to create natural glass.

Fireflies

In the early evening hours of the summer months, backyards and natural places all over the world light up with the enchanting dance of the fireflies. Also called lightning bugs, these creatures have "lanterns" attached to their tail portions that glow in a soft yellow-green tone.

While observing the fireflies, you may notice that the sequence of lights varies from specimen to specimen. Where one may light its tail portion three times quickly, another may light its tail twice slowly. Each firefly searches for a mate whose tail lights in the same pattern as its own.

Once fireflies reach adulthood, they do not feed. They spend the rest of their lives (on average, about two weeks) searching for a mate and reproducing.

Sadly, the fireflies are locked in a battle for their lives. We are rapidly losing the current population due to chemical sprays, compounded by global warming. The firefly could wind up extinct within the next few years and may cease to exist except as a magical memory.

The Phoenix

The myths of the phoenix came about due to the natural solar eclipses and humanity's inability to explain them in the past. The amazing part of these myths is that during an eclipse, one can see the pattern of the wings in the sun's corona. The phoenix was called the bird of the sun.

The ancient Egyptians considered the phoenix to be an avatar of the sun god. When his life was over (which was originally estimated at 500 years and went up close to 100,000 years in later times), he would light himself on fire, only to be reborn from the ashes after a suitable resting period (also around 500 years). It was said that the fire smelled of cinnamon.

The spirit of the bird wraps its nest in myrrh and sacred leaves and molds it into the shape of an egg. It carries the egg to the temple of the sun god and flies away for its rest.

The phoenix was described as red and yellow, with a purple neck, and was considered the most magnificent bird. Only one phoenix was allowed to live at a time.

Not only could the ashes give renewed life to the phoenix, but they were reputed to bring humankind back from the dead as well. One emperor even dined on a bird of paradise as a substitute for the phoenix, hoping to achieve immortality, but he was murdered shortly after.

Ovid stated that the phoenix ate only frankincense and other odiferous gums. It was further speculated by others that the phoenix hid from humankind intentionally.

The phoenix spans almost all mythologies and is a much-loved symbol of everlasting life. It is seen as a sign of peace and prosperity.

The Eighth Chakra

To get a clearer understanding of the divine aspects of fire, and how it relates to us and as a spiritual connector at large, one only needs to know a bit about the eighth chakra, also called the star chakra or the Kundalini serpent.

The eighth chakra sits about one to two feet above the crown chakra. It is the divine connection to spirit and to the universe that is imbedded within each of us. While this chakra sits outside of our earthly bodies, it rests well inside of our spiritual bodies.

The eighth chakra rules the areas of divine love, selflessness, and compassion. Opening the eighth chakra enhances one's ability to stimulate out-of-body experiences. This chakra has the power to move us to a more universal spiritual awareness. It also holds accumulated karmic residue.

The eighth chakra is the gateway between life on Earth and life beyond Earth. It cleanses us of all that is human and transforms us into all that is spiritual. It is the final pinnacle of a human incarnation. It releases all of the old patterns we may have and makes way for a broader view of life.

Opening the eighth chakra is not something to be undertaken lightly. There is a reason this chakra is not as well-known as the others or as widely talked about. When you open this chakra, all that you are and have ever been will be instantly revealed, and so will any dark aspects of your psyche that you were unaware of. Total knowledge of the self does not allow room for ego or illusions.

Psychic abilities are placed in this chakra. While opening this chakra will connect you to the universe, it may also leave you feeling isolated from the rest of humanity. Once you open the eighth chakra, you may find it hard to tackle the problems of everyday life, because they seem so small and insignificant. Financial concerns and household problems take a backseat to more global problems like starving children and war. And forget about listening to your girlfriends complain about how their partners don't understand them!

The color related to the eighth chakra is ultraviolet light, which is invisible to the human eye. Corresponding colors are emerald green and purple. This chakra rules the aura and the electromagnetic field. The eighth chakra represents infinity. Clear quartz corresponds to this chakra for healing purposes.

When the eighth chakra comes to life, even before it is purposefully opened, people undergo a "changing." The psychic gifts they have are amplified, and they may begin to see ghosts or hear strange voices from time to time. Most often, people don't realize what is happening, so they question their sanity.

Quick flashes of lights or movement perceived through the corner of the eye may begin to manifest. You may also have the experience where you feel a person's vibration enter the room, but when you look, no one is there. When I first began the process, a voice yelled my name in my ear and woke me up from a sound sleep. Apparently, I was not paying attention to what it was trying to tell me. The funniest thing is that it was the ear that was resting on the pillow that was yelled into. The strange symptoms of "changing" usually take several years to fully manifest, giving a person plenty of time to adjust, but they can be quite alarming.

Hearth and Home

The hearth or chimney has always been considered to be the most sacred spot in the home. The mere act of touching a chimney is said to bring good luck. However, if using a chimney for the first time, take care that you do not do so on a Friday. Also, never allow the fire to burn out unintentionally.

Never point into the fireplace or spit in it; to do so is rude to the household spirit that lives there. Only members of the household should be allowed to stoke the flames; to do otherwise would insult the resident guardian of the home.

In days of old, it was considered proper to bless the fireplace and chimney. This is best done before taking up residence in the home. The ceremony usually included symbols traced onto the hearth with holy water, as well as a sprinkling of salt upon the bricks.

It was said that a fire that burns too strongly in a fireplace is an omen of a violent argument. If a cinder should shoot forth from a roaring fire, it could be used for divining purposes. If it was heart-shaped, it predicted love. If it was purse-shaped, it predicted riches. If it was hollow and round, it predicted pregnancy. Beware of the coffin-shaped cinder, as it was thought to predict death.

It has been said that a fire should be lit by only one person at a time. If any two people choose to light it together, it is almost guaranteed that they will quarrel soon. Some old folklore goes far enough to say that a fire will never catch when in full view of the sun, for the sun is jealous and does not appreciate being mimicked. But if a fire takes hold quickly, it is a portent of visitors coming soon. If it burns more prevalently on one side of the fireplace, it predicts a wedding.

If the fire crackles loudly, it is a sign of cold weather to come. It is considered the worst taste to allow anyone to take a flame from the home fire on the new year. To do so assures that bad luck and hard times will follow throughout the year. Also at the new year, shadows cast by the fire are checked in order to make sure everyone is healthy. It was said that if the shadow appeared odd-shaped or shorter than the person, it was a sign of death. Soot falling from the chimney promises money to come, unless it happens during a wedding, in which case it predicts an unhappy marriage. If it falls on a fire gate, it means visitors will be arriving shortly.

The hearth symbolized the center of the home and the family. The Greek goddess Hestia, known to the Romans as Vesta, ruled over the hearth and all things domestic. She was considered to be the most gentle of the Olympians, but she preferred to spend her time on Earth with the mortals.

The Romans celebrated Vesta each year on June 9 with a festival called Vestalia. Vestal virgins tended her eternal flame in her temple.

According to Italian folklore, a race of fairies called Fireplace Folletti lived in the hearth. They were known to entrance new brides and make them despondent.

Djinn

The race of Djinn are said to have been created from a smokeless fire. The Arabian myths mention that the Djinn are fire spirits and have fire instead of blood running through their veins. The Djinn have great magical powers. It is thought that they can be captured or deflected with iron.

While they are most often portrayed as malevolent, there are good and bad creatures of this race. The good ones are said to be astoundingly beautiful. The Djinn are credited with "singing" oasis mirages into being and thereby tricking humankind. They also trick humans by shapeshifting into animals. It is thought that they wield some sort of supernatural control over humans and can influence their decisions and thoughts.

The Koran states that some Djinn are snakes. If they enter your house in this form, you are to put them out and warn them not to return, three times. If they enter your house a fourth time, you are advised to kill them. The Djinn are not immortal.

FIRE MAGIC

Fire magic is dramatic, entrancing, and magnificent. Fire Witches have a distinct preference for the more challenging magical tasks and full-fledged rituals. However, there are many simpler ways to use fire magic.

Always follow commonsense safety rules when working with fire.

CANDLE MAGIC

Primary to fire magic is the simple art of candle magic. When using candle magic, select a candle color that corresponds to your intent. There are many charts giving versions of candle correspondences, but the key to effective candle magic is to choose a color that you think suits the task. It's best to search for your own set of color correspondences. If you end up using a recommended color that doesn't calm you (if that is what is called for in the spell), how will it work to calm the universe? Here are the most commonly accepted color correspondences:

Black: Black is absorbing and can remove negative influences.

Blue: Blue is the color of the throat chakra. It is often used in circle casting to represent the western point. Blue works magically in matters involving health, protection, and inspiration and is known for its calming influence.

Brown: Brown can also be used in circle casting as a representation of the northern point (instead of green). Magically, brown works best in matters of grounding, forming a sturdy foundation, and special favors.

Gray: Gray is used for Otherworld communications and in legal matters.

Green: Green is the color of the heart chakra. It is often used in circle casting to represent the northern point. It works magically in matters involving money, fertility, growth, abundance, and nature.

Orange: Orange is the color of the navel chakra. It works well in matters involving ambition and success.

Pink: Pink is the universal color of happiness. It works well in matters involving beauty, love, friendship, harmony, marriage, romance, youth, and gentleness.

Purple: Purple is the color of the third eye chakra. It works best in matters involving spirituality and intuition.

Red: Red is the color of the root chakra. A red candle is often used in circle casting as the southern point. Red is used magically in matters involving passion, lust, sex, strength, anger, fast action, power, and charisma.

Yellow: Yellow is the color of the solar plexus chakra. It is used in circle casting to represent the eastern point. Magically, yellow works well in matters involving wisdom, knowledge, mental matters, joy, laughter, and memory.

White: White is neutral and suitable for any purpose. This is the color of the crown chakra.

Once you have selected the proper candle color, you must prepare the candle for magic:

1. Cleanse and consecrate the candle to the four elements.

2. Bless and anoint the candle with an appropriate oil.

3. Channel your magical intent into the candle. You may wish to bind it there with a ribbon or thread. Hair (even though it smells horrible when burnt) works very well to bind intent. You can carve symbols into the wax to further seal intent.

4. Light the candle. The flame releases the energy you programmed into it out into the universe to bring the desired change.

Herbs are often used in conjunction with candles to provide a little extra oomph. Specialty candles can also pack a powerful magical punch. Practitioners of Voodoo, Hoodoo, and Santería make use of these in magic and in offerings. The most common candle figures and their corresponding magical uses are as follows:

Black cat: The black cat candle is said to improve luck, especially in gambling matters.

Bride and groom set: These come in several colors. Red is used to elicit passion, pink to bring about reconciliation, white to attract new love, and black to break up a relationship. Male and female images are used as poppets and are chosen according to color.

Novena: Novena candles are used to honor spirit. Frequently, a novena is burned as an eternal flame until it burns itself out.

Seven-knob candle: The seven-knob candle is used for a seven-day spell. Each knob is assigned a specific task, and the candle is allowed to burn away one knob each day.

Skull: Skull candles come in several colors as well. Black is used for negative magic, and white is used for healing and protection and to remove negative influences. Red is used in relationship magic, and green is used for matters of money and luck.

Divining Candle Flames

Anytime you light a candle for a magical purpose, you can divine the wax, flame, and smoke patterns to interpret your answers. One simple but effective method is to assign the candle right and left sides that correspond to yes and no. If the candle drips first to the left and you assigned that side to no, then your answer is no.

Other methods call for watching the flame dance or the smoke spiral in a direction. If it dances to the west, you must watch your emotions. If it dances to the east, you must use your mental processes. Likewise, if it dances to the north, you will face a physical task, and if it dances to the south, you will have an intense experience of success.

If the flame burns high and strongly, the magic is working quickly and will be successful. If it is burning low and almost smothering itself out, you need to cleanse the entire area, including yourself, and rework the spell. If the flame is crackling, it means the magic has encountered opposition. If it burns mostly blue, it means you are connected to the divine. If it is sparking, it means to expect company.

If the soot around the candle turns the glass very black (like in a novena), it is thought to mean that someone has been thinking ill of you. A cleansing of the area should be performed. If the black soot is only around the top edge of the novena, it means that the magic has encountered opposition and may take a while to take effect.

If the smoke spirals toward you, the spell will work quickly. If it drifts away from you, you will have to persevere in order for your wish to be granted.

Some schools of thought teach to never blow out a candle flame, because it is rude to the elemental spirits of the fire. Others teach never to pinch them out. Likewise, some teach to never use matches and others say to use only matches. These are things you should decide for yourself. I personally have no problem with blowing out the flames, as fire depends on air to exist. Also, when employing candles for magic, always allow them to burn themselves out, if possible.

VINEGARS

Historically, magical vinegars have a long pedigree. The infamous Four Thieves Vinegar has been used in Voodoo and Hoodoo for ages. Vinegar imparts a fiery essence. It can cleanse any object and absorb negative vibrations.

Four Thieves Vinegar

This liquid is used as a hexing agent. Write your problem on paper, and soak the paper in the vinegar. Allow it to dry and then burn it to be rid of the problem.

To make Four Thieves Vinegar, take a bottle of apple cider vinegar and add the following herbs in handfuls:

Rosemary
Wormwood
Rue
Camphor (optional)
Patchouli

Heat the mixture to the point of almost boiling once a day for four days in a row. Strain and cap it tightly. Store in a cool, dark place.

Sour a Situation

Mix lemon juice and vinegar in equal portions. Write the situation you wish to sour on paper, and soak it in the liquid. Dry and burn. Another option that works very well is to use urine and vinegar.

The following vinegars are edible. They impart a zingy taste to foods as well as the magical properties of the herb used. They make wonderful salad dressings. When you reach the rebottling stage, it is proper to perform a blessing on the item, asking that it impart its magical energies with every drop consumed.

Healing Vinegar

3 cloves garlic, peeled and chopped
5 cayenne peppers, chopped
2 cups white vinegar

Combine the ingredients in a sealed jar and set it out in the sun to brew for two full days. Then take the jar inside and allow it to rest for two weeks. At the end of two weeks, you may strain and rebottle the vinegar.

Blessing Vinegar

½ cup rosemary
½ cup bay leaves
½ cup basil
½ cup sage
3 cups red wine vinegar

Combine all ingredients in a sealed jar. Place it out in the sun to brew for three full days. Take the vinegar back inside and allow it to rest for a full moon cycle, culminating on the full moon. Strain and rebottle. Allow the new bottle to charge under the full moon.

Fresh Beginnings

1 lemon, cut into small wedges
½ cup fresh mint, chopped
2 cups white vinegar

Combine the ingredients in a sealed jar and set it out in the sun to brew for two full days. Bring the jar inside and allow it to rest for two weeks. Strain and rebottle. You may garnish with fresh sprigs of mint and lemon peel twists.

MAGICAL BONFIRES

Magical bonfires are powerful. In the past they have been used to purify, remove bad luck and increase good fortune, bless, and destroy. Bonfires were traditionally jumped over to bestow upon the jumper the intent. In other words, in order to receive the blessings of good luck, one would jump across a fire that had been built to suit that purpose. They were also lit at certain times of the year to pay homage to the wheel of the year.

To use bonfire magic, you can cast your wishes into the fire and let the flames send the energy. You can do this by writing your intent on paper, sending it with vibrations, or placing a poppet in the flames. The following is a list of woods corresponding to magical intent:

For destruction: Yew and willow wood

For transformation: Holly, hazel, and hornbeam

For protection: Redwood and cedar

For power: Ebony, oak, and poplar

For healing: Ash, beech, and maple

For divination and scrying: Juniper, cedar, and sandalwood

Other magical effects can be obtained by using a particular type of wood or adding chemical compounds. Certain woods give off different colors of flame, and you can use these as the basis for a type of color magic. For instance, apple wood burns with rainbow-colored flames, while driftwood produces blue or lavender flames.

The best way to use coloring chemicals is to dissolve them in water and soak wood chips in the solution. (You may have to weigh down the wood chips by placing a brick over them.) Then sprinkle the wood chips on the fire. The chemicals and colors produced are as follows:

Yellow flames: Table salt

Purple flames: Potassium chloride

Orange flames: Calcium chloride

Blue flames: Copper chloride

Green flames: Copper sulfate

Red flames: Strontium chloride

Star Magic Meditation

Star light
Star bright
First star I see tonight
I wish I may

I wish I might
Have this wish I wish tonight

We all know the little rhyme that teaches how to wish upon a star. What we don't realize is the sheer power of the heavenly bodies of light. They shine so brightly that we can see them from Earth even though they are light years away. What looks to us to be only a twinkle is actually an energy force that is so strong that it can be considered unstoppable, at least by any human means.

The stars have been used in matters of wishing and intuition since the beginning of time. The gods are said to live among the stars, and the zodiac is based around those constellations.

Stars inspire inner journeys. To walk among them and obtain their powerful blessings, try the following meditation.

Light a white candle and a solar incense, such as cinnamon. Get comfortable. Slow your breathing to a deep, steady flow. Close your eyes. All around you is darkness. Sit comfortably in the darkness, enjoying the peace and quiet. When you are ready, get up and walk. As you stand up, you notice a twinkling far off in the distance. Begin to walk toward it. Focus on your breathing. As you move, you see more twinkling objects in the sky, and the area you are in becomes slightly brighter. Slowly walk until you are standing in the middle of a twinkling sky. Inhale and exhale. Sit and absorb the energies from each of these stars, listening to what they have to say. Keep your breathing deep, slow, and steady. As each star speaks, notice its vibration. These vibrations move along your chakras, clearing them and energizing them one by one. When you have heard all you wish and your chakras are clear and bright, stand and thank them all for their wisdom and energy. Inhale and exhale. Walk back to where you began your journey and sit down. Keeping your breathing steady, slowly open your eyes and come back to full awareness. Write down all that you learned in your journal.

Once you have performed the meditation, you will be energized by the power of the stars. You can use this energy for magical spells, if desired. If you have star-shaped candles or candle holders, these are excellent to release this special energy for manifesting goals. They also can help one attain that special connection in meditation the next time.

METAL MAGIC

In the same manner that the Earth Witch may specialize in rocks and crystals, the Fire Witch often has a preference for metal magic.

For centuries in most traditions, silver has been considered the metal of the Goddess, while gold has been seen as the metal of the God. This is partly due to their lunar and solar characteristics. Other metals correspond to the planets and the elements.

Metal contains magical energy. When worn or placed on the body, it can create a certain pattern of energy to manifest. For example, when performing a ritual to manifest money, placing a bit of gold on the altar or body creates a universal pattern of "like attracting like" and helps set the intent of the spell more firmly in the mind of the practitioner. The various magical metal correspondences are as follows:

Silver: Silver is the metal of the Goddess and the moon. It is also the metal of water. Witches hold silver as sacred. Silver works best in matters involving intuition, wisdom, dreams, love, peace, protection, and travel.

Gold: Gold is the metal of the God and the sun. Its element is fire. Gold works well in matters involving money, healing, power, protection, and success. Gold rings are said to be particularly useful in healing sties.

Brass: Brass is also a metal of fire and the sun. It works well in matters involving healing, money, and protection. It is often used on altars.

Copper: Copper belongs to the element of water and the planet Venus. It works well in matters involving luck, healing, love, protection, and money.

Iron: Iron is ruled by Mars and fire. It is powerful for negative or defensive magic. It is also grounding and known to keep fairies away. It is very protective.

Tin: Tin is ruled by Jupiter and air. It increases good luck and attracts money.

Lead: Lead is ruled by Saturn and earth. It works well in matters involving protection and in defensive or negative magic.

Aluminum: Aluminum is ruled by Mercury and air. It works well in matters involving communication, travel, and mental powers.

Pyrite: Pyrite is ruled by Mars and fire. It works best in matters involving money and luck.

PRISMS

Prisms have many magical uses. They are protective and self-cleansing. A charged prism can be used to manifest blessings, aid meditation, and dispel negative energies. Before you work with a prism for the first time, it will need to be cleansed of vibrations and consecrated to the elements. Then, it will need to be placed outdoors or in a sunny window to absorb solar energy for a full twenty-four hours.

If you wish to harness the protective properties of a prism, simply hang it, fully charged, around your neck or above a window. Prisms work wonderfully as protectors of the garden.

If you wish to dispel negative vibrations, simply hang a prism in the room where they linger, taking care that there is a light source behind the prism.

If you wish to use a prism for healing work or a shower-of-blessings type of spell, you can do so with a candle. Select a candle of the appropriate color (refer to "Candle Magic" at the beginning of this chapter) and hang the prism just above it. Allow enough space for the candle flame to grow large. As the flame releases the energies you programmed into the candle, the prism will reflect this energy and magnify it. When candles and prisms work together, the effect is instantaneous.

Meditating in the shower of colors produced by a prism can remind us to be thankful for our blessings. If you are feeling a bit off center, sit in a quiet place and allow the lights to dance on you. With each separate light, think of something that is right in your life, something that you are thankful for. In this manner, prisms remind us to appreciate what we have and to stay focused on the joy and happiness life brings.

Once you begin working with prisms, don't be surprised if it becomes a preference. Prisms are hard-working and easily cared for. To feed your prism, simply anoint it occasionally with a drop of honey. Allow it to soak up the honey for a few minutes and then rinse it in clear water.

MAGICAL LAMPS

Oil lamps have been used magically for many ages. They are usually marketed as hurricane lamps or kerosene lamps. Using a lamp is one of the easiest and most effective ways to harness the magical power of a flame. Because the bottom portion of the lamp is open, it is easy to fill it with magical herbs, stones, and other items to empower the oil, which is then distributed to the flame. If you create your own magical potions, you can add them to the oil base by the dram.

Magical lamps are safer to use than open candles on shrines, due to the glass cover over the burning flame, and they burn for long periods of time. They work wonderfully for honoring purposes. If you wish to have a lamp strictly for honoring a deity, keep it separate from the lamp you will be using for magical purposes. However, the lamp that is connected to deity can be used for celebrations, if desired, and in accordance with the wheel of the year.

To Attract Love

In the bottom portion of the lamp, where you pour the lamp oil, place a lodestone, a handful of rose petals, and a pinch of cinnamon. You may add food coloring to the oil, if desired. Place this lamp on an altar created with the intent of attracting love. Drape it with a pink cloth and place fresh flowers on it. On a small slip of paper, write exactly what you want and place it beneath the lamp. Burn a love-attracting incense, such as vanilla or rose. As you light the flame, state your desire. Light this lamp for at least one hour each day, until love manifests in your life.

To Promote Laughter and Joy

Add a citrine stone, a drop or two each of lemon and orange juice and peels of the rinds, and 3 drops of sandalwood essential oil to the base blend of the lamp oil. Place the lamp on an altar decorated with yellow and orange. Burn orange blossom incense. As you light the flame, state your desire. Burn this lamp anytime you wish to create a fun atmosphere.

For Protection

Place a tiger's-eye stone, a few flecks of black pepper, and a pinch each of blessed salt, basil, and cinquefoil into the base blend of the lamp oil. Place the lamp on an altar draped in white. Write the word "protection" on a small slip of paper and place it underneath the lamp. Burn herbal incense. Light this lamp daily for at least one hour to increase protection.

FIRE CORRESPONDENCES

Fire is considered masculine and projective.

Season: Summer

Magical virtue: To Will

Direction: South

Time of day: Midday

Sense: Taste

Fluid: Blood

Power animals: The phoenix, snakes, all manner of lizards, toads, dragons, tigers

Places of power: Deserts, tropical locations

Commonly associated colors: Red, orange, black

Linking items: Prisms, spears, lightning-bolt symbols, swastikas

FIRE STONES

Amber: Amber is well-known to increase luck, protect, and quiet nightmares. Amber heals the body, mind, and soul.

Apache tear: The apache tear is protective and draws good luck.

Banded agate: Banded agate is protective. It can be used as a storage facility for emotions and is also known to calm stressful situations.

Black agate: Black agate is protective and boosts courage.

Bloodstone: The bloodstone is so named because ancient warriors believed it had the ability to staunch bleeding. It was also said to be so powerful that it could destroy stone walls, gain victory in a war, and break bonds between people. It enhances physical strength. The bloodstone stands guard against evil and helps hold magic true to its purpose. I keep one on my altar at all times.

Carnelian: In ancient Egypt, carnelian was worn in rings to calm irritated tempers and dispel anger and jealousy. It is protective and healing and boosts courage. It is a grounding stone.

Citrine: Citrine is a cleansing stone. It protects and energizes and promotes joy and laughter.

Clear quartz: Clear quartz is an all-purpose booster. It can boost energy, magic, or anything. The energy contained in these stones is used to power small appliances. Clear quartz is a perfect conduit for magical energy and works in any situation.

Diamond: Diamond works well in matters involving protection, courage, marriage, healing, and strength.

Flint: The flint stone is protective and healing. In ancient times, flints were thought to be so protective that they were "fed" butter and beer.

Garnet: Garnet boosts strength and courage. It repels insects, heals the blood, and balances emotions. It is a regenerative stone.

Hematite: Hematite is a grounding stone. It balances the mind, body, and soul. It is very healing and boosts the psyche of anyone who is depressed or shy.

Lava: Lava rock is used for protection and healing. It is a symbolic representation of Pele, the Hawaiian volcano goddess.

Obsidian: Obsidian provides peaceful vibrations, helps with grounding, and makes a wonderful scrying surface. It is said to be impossible to tell a lie while wearing obsidian. This stone removes negativity and blocks aggressive magical attacks.

Onyx: Onyx is used primarily for protection. It also works to decrease sexual desire and in defensive magic.

Red agate: Red agate promotes a feeling of tranquility and peace. It has a calming influence. It stabilizes the aura and cleanses the psyche.

Red tourmaline: Red tourmaline is a balancing stone. It also is known to stimulate creativity.

Ruby: The ruby is cleansing and promotes lust. It protects against nightmares and increases joy.

Sulphur: Sulphur carries a negative electrical charge. It is absorbent and can remove negative vibrations. Sulphur can also be burned to re-create the very emotions that it absorbed.

Sunstone: Sunstone is a powerful aura and chakra cleanser. It increases energy and can be used to remove harmful influences.

Tiger's-eye: The tiger's-eye stone is protective, attracts money, promotes good luck, and enhances energy.

Topaz: Topaz works well in matters involving protection, money, and love. It is also worn to relieve depression, stress, anger, and fear.

Zircon: Zircon is used to promote peace, healing, love, and well-being. It can be used magically as a substitute for diamond.

FIRE HERBS

Allspice: Allspice is used to attract money and good fortune and in healing spells.

Angelica: Angelica is a very protective herb. It banishes all negative influences and promotes healing.

Asafaetida: This is a horrid-smelling herb. A tiny amount is used in rites of exorcism.

Basil: Basil removes all negative influences. It is protective and promotes love.

Bay: Bay leaves promote healing and intuition. They are protective and increase strength.

Black pepper: Black pepper is used to banish negative vibrations (especially jealousy) and entities. It is protective.

Cactus: The cactus is an extremely protective plant. It also absorbs negativity.

Carnation: Carnations are healing and protective and promote strength.

Chili pepper: The chili pepper promotes fidelity and love. It also works well in breaking hexes or curses.

Chrysanthemum: The petals of this plant are used for protection.

Cinnamon: Cinnamon attracts money, lust, success, healing, power, love, and good fortune.

Cinquefoil: Cinquefoil is used magically in matters involving purification, hex breaking, protection, money, and sleep.

Clove: Clove attracts money and love. It also is protective and is used in exorcisms.

Copal: Copal is a resin added to purification and love incenses. It is also used to represent the heart in poppets.

Coriander: Coriander works well in matters involving health and love.

Cumin: Cumin will protect any item from theft if placed nearby. It also works well in matters of fidelity and purification.

Curry: Burning curry increases a force field of energy for protective purposes.

Damiana: Damiana has the effect of increasing energy and lust and promoting love.

Dill: Dill is used to increase love, lust, and protection and to attract money.

Dragon's blood: Dragon's blood resin is a power booster. It is protective and promotes feelings of love and well-being.

Fennel: Fennel is best used in matters involving protection, healing, and purification.

Flax: Flax increases beauty, warmth, and intuition and promotes healing and protection. It also attracts money.

Frankincense: Frankincense has a long history of magical use. It is considered to be one of the most noble substances known to humanity. It is used to honor the sun, to promote spirituality, in matters of protection, and in exorcism rites.

Galangal: Galangal, also known as Low John the Conqueror, is carried for protection, placed in charm bags to attract money, powdered and burned to break any spells or curses, and sprinkled about to promote lust.

Garlic: Sacred to Hecate, garlic is used to protect, heal, and promote lust and in exorcism rites. It is used in the same manner as cumin to protect items from theft. It is absorbent and will remove negative vibrations.

Ginger: Ginger is a good substitute for galangal. It increases personal power and draws money and success.

Ginseng: Ginseng increases energy, brings wishes and beauty, promotes healing, love, and lust, and is protective.

Goldenseal: Goldenseal is a purifying herb. It also works in matters involving money and healing.

Hawthorn: Hawthorn increases happiness and promotes good will. It protects against lightning and guards chastity. It is sacred to the fairies.

Heliotrope: Heliotrope is used in exorcism rites and healing spells. It promotes wealth and intuition.

High John the Conqueror: This root is a tremendous power booster. It is suitable for any purpose and is known to balance emotions. It draws happiness, success, money, and love.

Holly: Holly attracts luck and good fortune. It is also protective.

Hyssop: Hyssop is a purification herb and is also protective.

Lovage: This herb is used extensively in love magic. It is also said to increase beauty.

Mandrake: Mandrake is used in poppet magic. It is protective and healing and increases money and love.

Marigold: Marigolds may be used to honor the sun by placing them on the altar. Magically, they work best in legal situations and in matters involving protection, dreaming, and intuition.

Masterwort: Masterwork increases personal energy and vitality when worn. It is protective and increases courage.

May apple: The May apple is the American substitute for mandrake. Its uses are the same.

Mullein: This herb is used in exorcism rites. It also works well in matters of protection, health, love, courage, and intuition.

Mustard: Carrying mustard seeds is thought to increase intellect and promote inner journeys.

Nutmeg: Nutmeg promotes fidelity, luck, and good health and attracts money.

Onion: The onion is absorbent and will remove any negative influences. It is healing and attracts money.

Orange: The orange is used in love magic and to increase money and luck.

Pennyroyal: Pennyroyal increases strength. It promotes peace and well-being and is protective.

Peppermint: Drinking peppermint tea will help one achieve a good night's sleep. It attracts love and healing and is said to boost intuition.

Pomegranate: Pomegranates are thought to bring about one's wishes and promote good luck when eaten.

Rosemary: Rosemary is a very important herb in magic. It is used to improve the memory, to protect, and to attract love and lust. It is healing and cleansing.

Rue: The aroma of rue is known to clear the thoughts. It is purifying and attracts love.

Saffron: Saffron is used to seek the aid of the winds, increase love and good fortune, and encourage strength. It promotes healing and intuition.

St. John's wort: This herb is used to treat depression. It is healing and protective.

Sassafras: Carrying sassafras attracts money and good health.

Sesame: Sesame attracts money and lust.

Snapdragon: If you wear a snapdragon, it is said that no one can lie to you. It is protective. It automatically reflects any negative magic sent your way back to the sender.

Sunflower: Sunflower seeds are eaten to increase fertility. They are worn to protect and guard one's health. The flowers are often used in wish magic.

Thistle: Thistle is used to dispel and repel evil. It is healing and protective.

Ti: Sacred to the ancient Hawaiians, Ti leaves are used to protect and heal. One should not plant the red Ti in a garden, as it is sacred to Pele and known to cause bad luck.

Tobacco: Sacred to many Native American tribes, tobacco is used to promote healing and purification.

Venus flytrap: The Venus flytrap is used to banish problems and promote loving vibrations. It is protective.

Witch hazel: Witch hazel is used in matters involving beauty, chastity, and protection.

Woodruff: Woodruff attracts victory and money. It is protective.

Wormwood: Wormwood is used to call spirits, protect, promote love, and increase intuition.

Yucca: The yucca plant is thought to aid in shapeshifting. It is protective and cleansing.

14

FIRE GODS AND GODDESSES

PELE

Pele is the beautiful Hawaiian volcano goddess. She embodies the essence of fire. She is so renowned that she is still worshipped to this day even though she is an ancient goddess. She is said to still appear to people, most often as an old woman. The old woman approaches and asks for a cigarette. She then lights her cigarette with a flick of her fingers and disappears right before the person's eyes. Offerings are still made to this goddess daily. Rum, cooked chicken, and strawberries are thrown into the crater at Mount Kilauea in an effort to appease and honor her.

Pele is known as "she who shapes the land," because from her fiery eruptions the islands increase their land mass. She loves hard, plays hard, and fights hard. She lives to please herself, first and foremost.

Pele was a beauty who was known for her indulgence in fleshly pleasures. She is credited with discovering the Hawaiian islands because she ran away from her sister's fury after seducing her husband. The sister sent tidal waves after Pele, drowning out her fires. She settled in

Mount Kilauea because it was the only place high enough to get away from her sister's furious waves.

Pele had many lovers. She was easily angered, and when she was, she would hurl lava at her lovers, turning them to stone. She was a goddess of violence.

When Pele caught the attention of Lono in his aspect of Kamapua'a, a battle ensued that almost destroyed the islands. Kamapua'a was a demigod who presided over agriculture. He most often took the form of a pig. Kamapua'a approached Pele, and Pele rebuffed him saying, "You are but a pig," and she sent forth great flows of lava to go along with her cruel words. Kamapua'a retaliated by sending torrential rains to extinguish her fires. The two battled on and on until finally the other gods had to make them stop for fear that the land would become so waterlogged it would never again sustain fire. Pele, impressed by Kamapua'a's showing of courage, gave in to him and became her lover for a time. When a child was born from the union, Pele went back to her philandering ways.

Pele is a jealous goddess. Her main rival was Poliahu, the beautiful goddess of snow-capped mountains. The fire and ice battles that the two partake in are ongoing even today. Pele does not like to be bested and is known to throw tantrums when she is.

Her jealousy almost cost her a sister. Pele's sister Hi'iaka, the goddess of the hula, was her favorite. It happened that Pele assumed mortal form and met a young man named Lohiau. They spent three days of bliss together, then Pele took her leave. She promised Lohiau she would send for him.

When Pele returned to Mount Kilauea, she entrusted her sister Hi'iaka to go fetch Lohiau. Hi'iaka agreed to do so, but only if Pele would tend to her gardens while she was gone. Pele agreed and Hi'iaka set out on her way.

Hi'iaka ran into a few problems and it took her longer than she anticipated to reach Lohiau. By the time she arrived, Lohiau was dying from a broken heart. Hi'iaka approached Lohiau as he took his final breath. Not one to break a promise, Hi'iaka shoved Lohiau's spirit back inside his body and went forward on her task with the young man in tow.

In the meantime, Pele convinced herself that the two were taking so long because they were having a romantic affair. In a jealous fury, she sent forth huge clouds of black smoke to send the message to her sister that she knew what was going on and was angry. Hi'iaka, knowing her sister well, knew what she was thinking but continued on her way. Over the course of the journey, Lohiau fell in love with Hi'iaka and told her he loved her more than he did Pele. Hi'iaka would not hear of it and carried the man back to Pele anyway.

When she arrived, Hi'iaka found her gardens burned and destroyed. Pele had already condemned her, even though she was innocent. In a rage, Hi'iaka threw herself on Lohiau and made love to him right before Pele's eyes. Pele sent lava and burned Lohiau to death. Hi'iaka, who was as stubborn as Pele, refused to accept defeat and went down into the crater of Mount Kilauea and rescued the spirit of Lohiau.

In an effort to calm her sister, Hi'iaka persuaded Lohiau's best friend to take his place as Pele's lover. Pele readily agreed and allowed Hi'iaka and Lohiau to live in peace.

Pele has a benevolent side for those deserving. One story relates how she saved a young girl's family due to the girl's kind nature.

Pele was disguised as an old woman. She spied two young girls gathering food to feed their families. Pele went to the girls and told them she was hungry and had not eaten in days. The oldest girl was selfish and refused to share. The youngest girl sat the lady down in front of their fire and gave her some food. She fed the woman until there was no food left. The old woman stood and said, "Something terrible is going to happen. Wrap your home in a tapa tonight." Then she left. The oldest girl yelled at the youngest about giving away all of their food, but the youngest girl went home satisfied and happy that she had helped someone. That night she wrapped her home in a tapa, just as the old woman had told her to. Sure enough, the volcano erupted that night, and the only home spared was that of the youngest girl who had shared her food with Pele.

Pele's priestesses would cut their hair on the volcano's edge, throwing it down to her. It was considered a symbol of devotion. Pele's sacred flower is the Red Lehua. It was the first plant to grow over lava-laden lands. While she is not a feminist, Pele embodies all that feminism stands for. She displays iron will, raw power, bravery, and perseverance.

LOOWIT

The Klickitat tribe, a Native American tribe of the Pacific Northwest, relates the tale of another volcano goddess, Loowit. She was known as the spirit of Mount Saint Helens, the volcano in Washington state. She was originally an old woman, but the Great Spirit turned her into a beautiful, young maiden.

Loowit was thought of as a hag and not very pleasing to look upon, with scraggly hair. She lived on the natural rock formation called the "bridge of the gods." This natural bridge spanned the entire Columbia River and served to unite the two tribes that lived on either side of it. They would meet and socialize and trade furs or food on the bridge. Young children used to come into Loowit's camp and try to steal her fire. The Great Spirit had charged Loowit with guarding the fire, and she did not let anyone take it. Her original name was Loo-wit-lat-kla, which means "keeper of fire" or "fire mountain."

Finally, Loowit went to the Great Spirit and asked that she be able to give fire to the people. The Great Spirit agreed, and Loowit found herself welcomed into the villages with open arms. She tended the fires for all of the tribes along the Columbia River. One evening the Great Spirit came to visit Loowit and told her that since she was so faithful, he would grant her one wish. Loowit, tired of being alone, asked to be young and beautiful. The Great Spirit feared there might be trouble, but granted her wish anyway.

As the news spread about her ravishing beauty, there soon came a day when two young chieftains, brothers no less, both wanted to marry the beautiful Loowit. They met on the bridge to discuss it, but they could not reach a compromise and determined to go to war. Whoever won would take Loowit as his bride. This angered the Great Spirit, who immediately destroyed the bridge, plunging Loowit and her sacred fire into the river below. As the rocks fell into place in the river, they created rapids. The Great Spirit killed the two chiefs for starting a war between the two tribes and told all of the people to stay away from each other. He then turned the two young warriors into mountains, Mount Hood and Mount Adams. The beautiful Loowit was turned into the snow-covered peak called Mount Saint Helens. All three of the mountains are volcanic and have been heard rumbling their displeasure with the others, but it was Loowit who lost her temper and had an outburst that the modern world will never forget.

In May of 1980, Mount Saint Helens erupted, killing fifty-seven people and thousands of animals. The devastation spanned over seventy square miles. The smoke and ash (over five hundred tons of ash) flew as high as twelve miles into the atmosphere. A massive mudslide moved along the side of the crater, flowing at over three hundred miles an hour. The mountain lost one thousand feet in altitude from the rock that gave way when it erupted. The vibrational force was so strong when it exploded that it flattened trees up to fifteen miles away.

Since the explosion in 1980, Loowit is thought to have grown cold, to an extent. A glacier covers her mountain peak, some two hundred yards thick and approximately one hundred yards wide. It is said that she will not erupt again for at least another hundred years. Curiously enough, a red flower was the first to grow on Loowit's lava-covered lands.

Loowit demonstrates that beauty is ever changing, like the face of her once beautiful mountain. The fire source within the mountain never sleeps. She reminds us that the body is temporary, but the soul is eternal.

BRIGID

Brigid (pronounced Breed) is the Celtic goddess of fire, a solar deity. In Britain she is known as Britannia. She was so beloved that when Christianity came to the land, the people claimed she was the human daughter of a Druid and had been baptized by none other than Saint Patrick. She was adopted into the church and later became a saint in her own right. Her name means "bright one." Saint Brigid is the patron saint of Ireland and is still worshipped to this day. The ancient goddess and the Christian saint are firmly meshed into each other's myths and legends.

Brigid is the daughter of the Dagda (the god of fertility) and the Morrigan. She was born at dawn, with a flame crowning her head and connecting her to the universe. Her special day is February 1 or 2 and is celebrated as Imbolc or Candlemas. Cows and female sheep were especially sacred to her. Her colors are white, black, and red. Her symbol is a widdershins-directed solar cross. Also sacred to her is the apple. It was said in legends that she owned a magical apple orchard and the bees would travel thousands of miles to feast on the nectar.

Originally, Brigid was a triple goddess, but not in the typical maiden, mother, and crone aspects. Her triplicity was found in her attributes. She ruled over inspiration, healing, and metal work. She wore shoes made of brass and hung her clothing on sunbeams. An eternal flame in her honor was watched over by nineteen priestesses, and on the twentieth day, she would tend it herself.

Brigid tends the forge and watches over the blacksmiths. She is credited with creating the magical art of metal smithing. According to some folklore, it was Brigid who created Excalibur, King Arthur's sword. Brigid also guards the home and hearth and watches over babies and animals.

Brigid was a fair goddess. One story relates that two men, both with a dreaded skin disease, approached her for healing. She told them to bathe themselves in her well. The first man did as he was bid and was cured. Brigid told him, "Now you must bathe your friend." The man replied that he could not, for fear of being contaminated again. Brigid said, "Then you are not truly healed," and gave him back the disease. She went on to say, "Return to me when you learn compassion, for you will find your healing there."

The Celtic societies attributed the changing of the seasons to Brigid (known in those particular legends as Bride) and the Cailleach. In the winter, Bride was imprisoned in an icy mountain. She managed to escape and brought spring with her. Corn dollies were often made in Brigid's likeness and carried by young girls from home to home as a blessing to the inhabitants. Those who lived in the house would in turn provide a donation. Later, the girls would take the dolly home and put her to bed while calling to Brigid that her bed was ready. There was hope that Brigid would enter the home and bestow her blessings upon the family, thus assuring their prosperity. This tradition is continued to this day on Imbolc.

Brigid was well-known for her charity work. She watched over agriculture and abundance. She was also a warrior goddess. She carried a spear and was ever willing to defend the home and hearth. She encouraged women to stand up for themselves and fight for their rights.

The American tradition of Groundhog Day is a cousin of Imbolc. Originally, in Ireland, it was Brigid's snake appearing from its mound that determined the weather prediction.

LOKI

Loki is the Norse god of fire. He was not born a god, but a giant, the natural enemy of the gods. Through a blood oath with Odin, Loki gained the powers of a god and was able to live in Asgard.

Loki fathered several children. Among them were Hel, the goddess of death, Fenrir, the giant wolf, and Jormungand, the serpent.

Loki is credited with gifting Thor with Mjolnir, the magical hammer. He had angered Thor by playfully cutting his wife's hair. Thor's wife, Sif, was renowned for her beautiful blonde hair. In order to spare his own life, Loki went to the dwarves and asked them to fashion Sif a wig of gold. While he was there, he commissioned the hammer for Thor. But, out of spite, he hit the dwarf during its creation, resulting in a handle that was too short. Nevertheless, the hammer was sacred and a most prized possession. Loki also presented Odin with his magical ring and his spear. These he commissioned from the same dwarves, promising his head as payment. The dwarves readily agreed and created the magical items Loki had ordered. When it came time to pay, Loki said, "You may have my head, but you may not have any part of my neck." This left the dwarves without payment, and they knew it. Furious at being cheated, the dwarves sewed Loki's mouth shut in an effort to prevent any further lying. Loki was the proverbial "silver-tongued devil" and could talk his way into and out of most situations. He was thought to be very handsome.

Loki was a trickster god. He was a shapeshifter. None of the other gods liked him, but because of his blood bond with Odin, he was tolerated, until the time came when his actions demanded retribution. He was responsible for the death of Balder.

Legends relate that Balder was the son of Odin and Frigg. He was the god of light, and his twin brother, Hod, was the god of darkness. Hod was born blind.

Frigg had a terrible dream that her beloved son Balder was about to meet a dreaded fate, so she walked the entire Earth asking every single thing to promise not to harm Balder. As a result, Balder became invulnerable. The gods would amuse themselves by hurling arrows and stones at him, only to laugh as each thing was deflected. Not even fire could hurt him.

Loki shapeshifted into an old hag and went to visit with Frigg. Over the course of the conversation, he asked if there was any thing from which Frigg had not been able to extract a promise of protection. Frigg revealed that yes, there was one thing: mistletoe. Frigg thought there was no way mistletoe could harm her son, so she did not make that plant swear an oath to her. The old hag nodded and said no more.

One day the gods were gathered about, playing their usual game of trying to harm Balder, when Loki asked Hod, who had never participated, to play. Hod replied that he had never done so because he was blind and could not see. Loki loaded up a mistletoe arrow and guided Hod's arm so that he could join in the revelry. When the arrow hit Balder, he immediately fell dead and his soul went to Hel's domain.

Frigg was devastated. She pleaded with Odin to return her son to her. Hermod volunteered to go to Hel and try to ransom Balder away. He rode away on Odin's famed eight-legged horse, Sleipnir. Hel said she would release Balder if the world needed him badly enough that every single thing wept for his return.

Frigg again walked the Earth asking every thing to weep for her son, so that he may come home. Loki changed himself into the giantess Thokk. When Frigg asked him to cry for her son, he replied, "Let Hel keep what she has." Hel refused to release Balder.

When the gods found out that Loki was responsible for Balder's death, they went searching for him to bestow justice. True to his nature, Loki ran and hid. He changed himself into a salmon and eluded the net the gods had placed to capture him. Just as he was about to jump over it and flee to the sea, Thor grabbed him by the tail. Thor and the other gods took Loki to a cave. They transformed Loki's son Vali into a wolf and ordered him to kill another of Loki's sons, Narfi. They took Narfi's innards and tied Loki to a rock in the cave. Then they placed a giant snake above him that dripped an acidlike venom on him. The venom was so painful that when it landed, it caused Loki to have convulsions, which manifested in the form of earthquakes. It is said that Loki will remain there until the final battle, commonly known as Ragnarok. When Ragnarok begins, it is said that Loki will lead the giants against the gods.

HELIOS

Helios is the Greek god of the sun. He was often referred to as Helios Panoptes, which means "Helios, the all-seeing." He drove his bright chariot across the skies daily, led by four horses. They were called Eos, Pyrois, Aethon, and Phlegon. Helios was depicted as a youthful god with short hair and a bright halo. He wore a cloak and carried a globe and a whip.

Helios fathered Phaeton ("the shining one"). Ovid relates that Phaeton was being teased at school, because no one believed he was truly the child of a god. Phaeton had never met his father and went to his mother demanding to meet him so that he might know for sure. His mother gave him directions to the land where his father dwelled, and with that, Phaeton was off.

When he found the palace of the sun, his eyes beheld a sight richer than any he could have dreamed. The palace was glittering with gold and precious jewels. Phaeton climbed the stairs, opened the huge silver doors, and stepped inside. He walked toward his father, but had to stop because the light was too bright.

Helios asked what his purpose was, and Phaeton replied, "I am Phaeton. I seek proof that you are my father." Helios walked to the boy and embraced him. He said, "I am your father, and to prove it, ask whatever you wish and it will be granted." Phaeton asked to one day drive the chariot across the sky. Helios recanted his promise. He said, "This is the one promise I must deny. It is not safe—you are a mortal. The path is steep and treacherous. None but myself can drive the chariot of the day safely. Beware my son, as it would be a fatal gift. You want proof of my blood? See my concern. Would I care if you were not of me? Choose anything else and it will be yours."

Phaeton persisted. Helios replied sadly, "I gave my oath and must keep it, but I beg of you to choose something else." Phaeton insisted on driving the chariot. Helios reluctantly led the way.

Before the gate was opened, releasing the chariot, Helios begged his son, "At least heed my advice. Spare the whip and hold tight to the reins. Keep to the middle path—it is the safest. Please reconsider and stay here and be safe." Phaeton jumped in the chariot and grabbed the reins. He called out his thanks to his father and was off. The horses moved so quickly that Phaeton was alarmed. He realized that he could not control the horses. The chariot, lighter than normal, was tossed hither and yon as Phaeton struggled to stand. Then—horror of horrors—Phaeton noticed that the chariot had left the traveled road and was running blindly through the sky.

He was white-faced with terror and wished he had listened to his father and stayed at the palace. He dropped the reins as he trembled with fear. The horses, sensing their freedom, dashed about unrestrained. They ran too close to the Earth, burning crops and destroying cities. Areas became deserts under the intense heat. The world was on fire.

Zeus, left with no other choice, hurled a lightning bolt at Phaeton in order to stop the chariot's wild ride and save the Earth. Phaeton fell from the chariot with his head on fire and landed in a river. Helios had lost his son.

Helios also fathered Circe, Aeetes, and Pasiphae. He was the grand-father of Medea and also of the Minotaur. He was the inspiration for the sunflower, although it is a sad tale.

A young water nymph named Clytie fell madly in love with the bright Helios. Alas, Helios did not return her feelings. Clytie, in her heartbreak, sat on the cold ground pining away for her love. For nine days she sat, not eating or drinking, simply watching Helios make his rounds across the sky. Her lovely upturned face followed his every move. Finally, she had sat so long that her body became rooted to the ground and her face transformed into a flower—a flower that always has its face turned to the sun.

In the *Odyssey*, Homer relates that Helios was the first to know of the affair between Ares and Aphrodite. The two would meet in secret under the very nose of Aphrodite's husband, Hephaestus. Helios told Hephaestus what was going on, and he immediately set up a trap to catch the two lovers. When Hephaestus caught them, he invited all of the Olympians to come and see, embarrassing Ares and Aphrodite.

RE

Re, sometimes called Ra, is the Egyptian sun god. He is the supreme god in the Egyptian pantheon. His main cult center was Heliopolis, but eventually he was accepted as a national god. He had many as-pects, varying with the time of day. In the evening he was called Atum-Re and was depicted as a man with a ram's head. At noon he was depicted as a solar disc. In the morning he was known as Re-Horakhty and was associated with the falcon god Horus and depicted as a scarab beetle.

Re was present in every stage of the ancient Egyptian's life. He walked the Earth as sunlight on the ground. He was in the heavens as the sun. He was in the Underworld at night, where he would regener-ate and prepare to be born again the next morning. He was the creator god and had emerged from primordial waters to design and bring life to every thing on Earth. He was considered both father and mother of all living things. Re was also considered to be the king of the Earth.

It was thought that Re had ruled on the Earth until he grew old and weary. Later, he ascended to the heavens to continue his reign.

In the Underworld, Re experienced a rather uncomfortable evening. In this aspect he was known as Auf. For twelve hours he had to supply sunlight to the tortured souls that lived in the Underworld.

The Egyptian creation myths assert that Re created himself and rose from the waters. He created all of the other gods and everything on Earth. It was said that humans were borne of his tears. To create something, Re had only to visualize it and speak its name.

Re took the form of a man and ruled the Earth as king. It was known as a time of plenty. As a human, after thousands of years, Re began to grow old. The people started to laugh at him, which infuriated Re. He paid closer attention and noticed that the men were doing things he did not approve of. They coveted his power and wanted to take his place. Re created Sekhmet to destroy those that would seek to overthrow him. Sekhmet was called the "eye of Re" and was considered to be his daughter. When she began her slaughter, she was so vigorous that Re began to worry that she would destroy all of humanity. She took such joy in the killing and drinking of blood. Re determined that to save humankind, he had to drug her and let her sleep off her fury. So, he tinted a large amount of beer red, and when Sekhmet found it she thought it was blood and proceeded to lap it up with delight. She fell into a sound sleep, and when she awoke, she was calm and sated.

A while later, Re discovered that his mind was not as sharp as it used to be. In human form, several thousands of years old, his advanced age had slowed down his mental faculties. He retained his power over Earth only by keeping his true name secret.

The wise Isis was known as a powerful enchantress. It was rumored that the only thing Isis did not know was the true name of Re. Ever eager to learn more and advance herself, Isis saw the elderly Re allow a bit of his spittle to drip onto the ground. She quickly scooped it up and fashioned the mud into a cobra—the first cobra ever to exist. She placed the cobra on a dusty roadside that Re traveled each day. When Re walked by, the cobra struck. Re cried out for help as the poison began to overtake him. Isis came to him and told him she would heal him, but that in order to do so she must know his secret name, as it was the only thing powerful enough to cure him. Re, after much pain and subsequent cajoling, cried out, "Let my heart carry my secret name to the heart of Isis! But it may be used only by her and her son." Isis swore it would be so. When the secret name manifested in her heart, she healed him. Re then took his place in the heavens, allowing Isis and her son to rule the Earth.

Over the course of time, Re's legends and attributes became merged with many other gods to create a sort of composite god. Eventually, the ancient Egyptians combined Re with Amun (another creator god) to form one ultimate creator god, Amun-Re.

15

COMBINATION SPECIALTIES

OPAL MAGIC

The opal holds the same properties as all four of the elements combined. It is an extraordinary stone and is unequaled in its magical power.

Superstitions abound about the opal. It is commonly thought that anyone who was not born in the month of October should not wear an opal, that it is unlucky and could possibly have dire consequences. This superstition came about because of a nineteenth-century novel, Sir Walter Scott's *Anne of Geierstein*. It is not based on the actual properties of the gemstone itself, but on a work of fiction.

While the opal has extremely strong magical characteristics, it is weak in physical strength. Do not use your opals in a manner that will bump them about or cause significant temperature changes. Opals are very delicate and will crack or shatter. Black opals and fire opals are highly prized as magical stones.

Because the opal carries the attributes of all four elements, it may be used for any intent as long as you keep one thing in mind: it is a magnifier. Whatever you use it for will manifest in many different ways, and so will any backlash you might earn if using an opal for negative work. Because the opal is a blend of colors and carries the attributes of each one within it, it is unlimited in its magical uses.

The best use for an opal is as a guardian for protection. Keep it as a positively charged energy booster, use it as a scrying vehicle, or use it as a stone to contact divinity. Also, a charged opal placed on the third eye is a powerful kick to encourage astral projection.

Opal Protection Spell

Light a white candle and place the opal at the base of it. Say:
> *Flashing lights*
> *Rid me of fright*
> *A guardian I do seek.*
> *Protect all you see*
> *Home and family*
> *It will be as I speak!*

RAINBOW MAGIC

In many ancient belief systems, the rainbow served as a bridge between the planes of existence. It connected God and humans, but required death of the human body before one could cross it. The Hawaiians spoke of the god Lono utilizing the rainbow in this manner, while the Nordic version spoke of an icy bridge called Bifrost. The rainbow bridge was thought to be the footpath for the souls of the dead leading to their place of rest and regeneration.

In regions of the world below the equator, the ancient belief was that the rainbow was a serpent. The rainbow serpent was thought by many people to have been the creator of the world.

The rainbow is symbolic of love and commitment. It represents marriage in the traditional sense as well as being the symbol for gay pride. The rainbow signifies unity.

In modern times, we can utilize the rainbow by using color magic techniques. In the late 1800s, Dr. Edwin Babbitt introduced a form of color therapy called "rainbow healing" in his book *Principles of Light and Color*. He asserted that placing any liquid, even water, into the correct color of bottle or jar and then infusing that liquid with sunlight could have a healing effect on the body, if done properly. The healing water/color combination correspondences are as follows:

Red: Bladder, feet, legs, large intestines, male genitalia

Orange: Kidneys, small intestines, spleen, bones, spine, female genitalia

Yellow: Liver, gallbladder, stomach

Green: Lungs, heart, immune system

Blue: Throat, jaw, tongue, teeth, lips, saliva glands, lymph glands

Indigo: Eyes, ears, nose, sinuses, pineal gland

Violet: Hair, scalp, brain, pituitary gland

For magical work, a colored bottle or jar can add the unique vibration of its shade to spell concoctions. For example, if you were to make a love potion and place it in a pink or red bottle, the color tone would add additional magical vibrations to the potion ingredients.

There are no limits to working with this sort of magic—everything has a color. From your shade of clothing to empowered bath water, all of nature is inspired by color. We each have our own personal rainbow in the form of our chakras: red, orange, yellow, green, blue, violet, and white. The only difference in the accepted color schemes is that we consider our crown chakra to be white, and the sixth color of the rainbow is indigo.

Rainbow moonstones, opals, hematite, and all glowing or iridescent types of stones work particularly well in rainbow magic, as do prisms.

According to superstition, rainbows hold one of the most unique attributes found in magic: the power to levitate. The mysterious force of evaporation was explained by the ancient people as the rainbow drinking all of the available water. Sailors thought that a rainbow could actually drink a whole ship. These superstitions give a rather sinister view of the rainbow. On the opposite side of the spectrum, there are legends that relate that the rainbow is a reminder of good things to come from divinity, a blessing, and a portent of peace. So, what is a rainbow actually good for magically?

Taking the myths out of the equation and looking at the rainbow from a strictly elemental point of view, the rainbow is the result of air, water, and fire. Air is about the mind, water is about the emotions, and fire is about the soul. Hence, the rainbow is not about the physical body, but the energy body, which is why color magic works so well. The rainbow reminds us that while red and blue may be opposites in color, they each have a place in the overall composition of the color scheme.

When a rainbow is present, it is prime time for divination. Other intents that benefit from the presence of a rainbow are spells that work for beauty, trust, peace of mind, harmony, healing, and finding your place in life.

You can harness the power of a rainbow quite easily, and simple elementary-school science can teach you how to make a rainbow in your own yard. First, find a multicolored garter strap and place it on a white piece of paper. Take a large glass of water and place it between the sun and the paper. When the sun shines through the water, a rainbow will appear on the paper. While the garter lies there and soaks up the power of the rainbow, it is a good time to bless it and inform it of its duty.

Rainbow Meditation

With the following meditation, you can journey under the arc of the rainbow to discover what Mother Nature has in store for you.

Begin by setting your altar with materials that will help you focus on the goal at hand. Make sure you do this in sacred space. Place bright colors on the altar, with at least one candle. Burn a floral incense. Relax and take five deep, long breaths. As you exhale, breathe out all of the day's stress. As you inhale, take into yourself confidence for the journey ahead and the divine love of all of the universe. Close your eyes.

Everything is dark. Slowly, you realize you are standing in a vast forest. The birds chirp and the butterflies dance all around you. The forest smells fresh, like after a spring rain. You walk toward a clearing. The sky is getting lighter and you are filled with wonder and peace. As you walk into the clearing, you see a beautiful crystal-blue lake. There is a rainbow standing with one leg in the lake and the other leg somewhere in the forest. You walk under the arc of the rainbow and sit. You are washed in color. A refreshing breeze blows your hair away from your face, and you are content to just be in the moment. Just on the other side of the arc, you see a woman dressed in white, with flowers in her hair. She walks slowly toward you, radiating peace and love. She whispers to you all of the things you will accomplish in this life, secrets about what you are meant to do.

When you have heard all you wish, thank her and walk back toward the forest. By following the butterflies, you reach the spot you were in before. Sit and close your eyes, happy and content. Open your eyes and find yourself back in your body at the present time. Write down all that you learned in your book of shadows or in a meditation journal.

Rainbow Brew for Peace

Combine nine each of the following flower blossoms:
> Red rose
> Orange marigold
> Sunflower
> Chicory
> Iris

Place these blossoms in a clear jar, and add enough oil to just cover the flowers. Allow it to sit in a sunny window for three full days and nights, then strain. You may use the oil to anoint objects when working for peace.

Rainbow Potion for Happiness

Take a glass of spring water and add a squeeze of orange juice to it. Pour the solution into an orange bottle. Allow it to sit for three days. Pour the water out of the orange bottle and into a yellow one. Add a squeeze of lemon juice. Allow it to sit for three days. Take the water into a brightly lit place and say, "By the power of the sun, I do will that this potion instill my entire being with happiness, laughter, and joy. So mote it be!"

STORM MAGIC

Rain, rain
Go away
Come again
Some other day.

Humankind has attempted to control the weather for hundreds of years. As we have yet to gain any sort of control, storm magic proposes that we instead merge energies with the storm, and harness its natural power to bring about changes we desire.

At any given moment, there are hundreds of storms covering the face of the Earth. Visualizing ourselves as part of the storm allows us to tap into its energy force. Certain colors can help attune the conscious mind to the storm. Gray, indigo, black, and other "rainy-colored" candles or clothing can help set the mood for merging energies. Avoid bright, sunny colors when using storm magic, as they tend to break up the cloud gatherings in the mind and impede focus.

If the storm is local to you, you can make use of it in a more practical and immediate manner. For example, you can place special items outside so that they may soak up the furious energy. Likewise, you may wish to catch some of the storm water, as it is potent and electrically charged.

Storm magic serves the primary functions of cleansing and charging. Storms include all four of the elements, depending on the type of storm and overall strength. In the Middle Ages, farmers believed that the crops would not yield fruit if there was not a thunderstorm at the beginning of the summer. When viewed in that manner, the thunderstorm is seen as nurturing.

Magical jewelry that is cleansed and charged through the power of a storm can contain massive amounts of raw energy. Crystals and stones can also benefit in the same manner. If you happen to catch a thunderstorm on the night of a full moon, the power of whatever you charge will be incredible. I recommend charging all of your tools if you are lucky enough to have this combination.

There are some stones that you cannot charge under the power of a storm, as they are thought to work against storms. They are as follows:

Agate: Agate works against storms and lightning.

Amethyst: This stone works against storms.

Beryl: Beryl calls rain but banishes storms.

Coral: Native Americans believe that coral halts foul weather.

Garnet: Garnet works against lightning.

Malachite: Malachite works against lightning.

Ruby: Ruby works against storms in general, and is also said to work against floods.

One particularly good stone for storm magic is the black opal. Alternatively, you may choose to visualize yourself as merging with the storm. Quietly churning, you absorb the transforming energy from the electrically charged clouds. You feel the winds and water dance against you, and as your pores open to receive the cleansing energy, you get a sudden surge of power. You have just harnessed the raw power of a storm. Channel it into whatever magical goal you have set for yourself at this time.

Other than cleansing, charging, and harnessing energy, what else can you do with Mother Nature's powerful dance? Storms are wonderful for banishing, honoring the divine, honoring yourself, regenerating the self, justice magic, and spells for success.

Water that falls from a storm is great for bathing tools, consecrating objects, asperging an area or the self, or to use in any water-based magical formula, such as potions and elixirs. You may, of course, drink the water to consume the power of the storm. But if you live in a polluted area, it might be best to avoid drinking it and instead use it for anointing purposes.

A thunderstorm is an ideal time for a devotional ritual or a simple prayer rite. It is also the perfect time to work for a transformation. Create a special altar with gray, indigo, and black candles, and use similar colors for the altar cloth. Place smoky-quartz chunks or geodes around the candles. If you have a mirror or reflective surface, place that underneath the candles for a lightning type of effect. Burn a rain-scented incense. Sit quietly for a few moments, attuning yourself to the storm. Chant:

> *The wind and water dance*
> *The fire flashes flame*
> *I am united with the storm*
> *Upon the earthbound plane.*

Once you feel connected, talk to the Lord and Lady. Tell them what you want to gain in life and what you hope to overcome. This is the perfect time to work for manifesting a change within yourself, so go deep into your thoughts and troubles. Spill it all. Think of it as therapy and let loose your inner storm.

After a thunderstorm, the world is infused with a powerful magical energy that is peaceful and refreshed. Draw this strength into yourself by collecting natural objects that the storm may have scattered. Leaves, acorns, and the like retain the boost of special storm energy and can add punch to your magical spells. Likewise, if you grow your own herbs for spell work, you may want to consider a small harvest at this time.

Stormy Success

Prepare your storm altar with gray, indigo and black candles. Place a single gold candle in the center of the altar. Burn a rain-scented incense. Meditate and call up the vision of the storm in your mind. Merge your mind to it and absorb the energy. Channel the energy into the gold candle with the intent of success. Say:

> *With the strength of the storm and the sun*
> *Today I see my will be done*
> *As lightning flickers, as the winds sing*

I call to myself success in all things
So mote it be!

Remove an Obstacle

Combine equal amounts of basil, black pepper, and salt in a mortar and pestle. Grind to a fine powder. Add 9 drops of storm water and place in a sealed jar. Allow the jar to sit outside during a thunderstorm. Write down on a piece of paper the obstacle you would like to remove from your life. After the storm, when the herbal mixture is fully charged, sprinkle it on the paper. Burn the paper and throw the ashes into the next storm.

ICE AND SNOW MAGIC

The primary purpose of ice magic is transformation. Ice is a combination of water and air. Once frozen, if fire is added, the ice melts.

Floating candles in a bowl of water and ice may seem like a simple type of spell, but it calls for a natural balance to take place. Moreover, writing your problems on paper and freezing them may also seem like a simple spell, but it is highly effective.

One of my favorite magical uses for ice is the "stop something in its tracks" type. In other words, after an argument, I am not above writing my aggravation down on paper and freezing the paper until such a time as I can comfortably deal with the problem. Once I'm ready, I simply thaw out the paper and deal with it. You can perform this type of magic for any sort of negative trait within yourself that you wish to be rid of.

Likewise, you can also manifest with ice. Place magnets or symbols into the ice and then allow the ice to melt as it removes any obstacles between you and your goal and releases the energy to bring you your wish .

Ice Tray Magic to Transform a Relationship

Serve your lover a drink over this special ice.

1 ice tray
Water, to fill the ice tray

Red food coloring
Red rose petals—2 for each compartment of the ice tray

Tint the water a light, pretty pink and pour it into the ice tray. Add two rose petals to each compartment while chanting this verse:

From fluid to solid
From water to ice
My relationship is as stable
As the rose does entice
What love was before
Is now twice
So mote it be!

Diet Ice

Use this method to empower the water to remove excess weight from your body.

1 ice tray
Water, to fill the ice tray
Yellow food coloring
Lemon wedges

Tint the water a pretty yellow and pour it into the ice tray. Drink water with a lemon wedge over this ice as part of your diet. Each time you add ice, affirm, "As the ice melts away, so too does my excess weight. So mote it be!"

FIRE AND ICE

When using fire and ice together, you are calling for a natural balance to take place. It can be a balance of the self, a balance of a situation, or even a balance of the checkbook.

Balancing the Self

A large, clear glass bowl
Equal amounts of water and ice
3 floating candles (these can be multicolored, gray, or brown)
Handful of salt

Place the ice in the bowl. Add the salt and say, "I cast off any negativity and purify this ice. It is blessed by the Goddess and God." Add enough water to make the surface smooth, and bless it in the same manner. Place the candles in the bowl and say, "I call upon my higher self to bring my being into harmony. I will myself to be balanced in all situations. So mote it be!" Clap your hands three times and light the candles. This is a good time to reflect on which areas of your life need balance the most. It also is a beautiful sight to sit and watch the ice melt while the flames dance. Spend an appropriate amount of time in reflection before you close your circle or leave the area.

Balancing a Situation

Calling a situation into balance can be a bit trickier. For example, suppose you lost your job due to a nasty rumor or some such thing, and the circumstances were entirely unjust. You can use fire and ice to call for a balance to the situation. You will need the following:

An empty paper milk carton (quart size)
Water, to fill the milk carton
A gray taper candle as tall as the milk carton
A pencil
Piece of string
Cooking spray

Spray the inside of the carton with cooking spray. Tie the string to the wick of the candle. Wrap the other end of the string around the pencil. Place the candle in the milk carton and use the pencil to hold it upright by placing the pencil across the top of the carton. (You may cut small notches in the top of the carton if needed.) Carefully fill the carton with water and place it in the freezer. When the water is frozen solid, tear the carton away. Place the candle in your cauldron over a layer of sand. Say, "I call upon the universal forces of my Lord and Lady to bring balance to my life. I will that my current job predicament be brought to a just result. So mote it be!" As you light the candle, visualize yourself working happily.

Snow magic works in a similar way, yet offers more options. Instead of making the typical snowman in your snowed-under yard, why not make a cosmic snow egg? Place the power to remove a bad situation inside the egg, and watch as it melts your problem away. Snow may also be used for manifesting, sometimes in the most delicious of ways, as in the following recipe.

Love Snow Cream

Fresh, clean snow
1 teaspoon vanilla extract (love)
Dash of salt (to purify)
½ cup sugar (to sweeten)
1 cup milk (blessings)
Chocolate syrup (lust)

Empower all the ingredients with positive energy. Mix together all except the snow. When thoroughly mixed, add enough snow to completely absorb the liquid. Place the snow cream in the freezer if you want a firmer treat. Garnish with chocolate syrup, and share with your lover in front of a roaring fire.

BIBLIOGRAPHY

Batmanghelidj, F., M.D. *Water: For Health, for Healing, for Life*. New York: Warner Books, 2003.

Beckwith, Martha. *Hawaiian Mythology*. Honolulu: University of Hawaii Press, 1976.

Bharadwaj, Monisha. *The Indian Luck Book*. New York: Penguin Compass, 2003.

Bluestone, Sarvananda, Ph.D. *How to Read Signs and Omens in Everyday Life*. Rochester, VT: Destiny Books, 2001.

Bonnefoy, Yves. *Greek and Egyptian Mythologies*. Chicago: University of Chicago Press, 1991.

Buckland, Raymond. *Color Magick: Unleash Your Inner Powers*. St. Paul, MN: Llewellyn Publications, 2002.

Bulfinch, Thomas. *Bulfinch's Greek and Roman Mythology: The Age of Fable*. Mineola, NY: Dover Publications, 2000.

———. *Bulfinch's Mythology*. New York: HarperCollins, 1991.

Campanelli, Pauline. *Ancient Ways: Reclaiming Pagan Traditions*. St. Paul, MN: Llewellyn Publications, 2001.

Clark, Jerome. *Unexplained!* Detroit, MI: Visible Ink Press, 1999.

Cunningham, Scott. *The Complete Book of Incense, Oils & Brews.* St. Paul, MN: Llewellyn Publications, 2001.

———. *Cunningham's Encyclopedia of Crystal, Gem & Metal Magic.* St. Paul, MN: Llewellyn Publications, 2001.

———. *Cunningham's Encyclopedia of Magical Herbs.* St. Paul, MN: Llewellyn Publications, 2001.

———. *Earth, Air, Fire & Water: More Techniques of Natural Magic.* St. Paul, MN: Llewellyn Publications, 2004.

———. *Earth Power.* St. Paul, MN: Llewellyn Publications, 1983.

———. *Hawaiian Magic & Spirituality.* St. Paul, MN: Llewellyn Publications, 2000.

Dugan, Ellen. *Garden Witchery: Magick from the Ground Up.* St. Paul, MN: Llewellyn Publications, 2003.

Garrett, J. T. *The Cherokee Herbal: Native Plant Medicine from the Four Directions.* Rochester, VT: Bear & Company, 2003.

Gleason, Judith. *Oya: In Praise of an African Goddess.* San Francisco: HarperSanFrancisco, 1992.

Graves, Robert. *Greek Myths.* London: Penguin Books, 1981.

Guiley, Rosemary Ellen. *The Encyclopedia of Witches and Witchcraft.* Second edition. Checkmark Books, 1999.

Franklin, Anna. *The Illustrated Encyclopaedia of Fairies.* London: Vega, 2002.

Hall, Judy. *The Crystal Bible: A Definitive Guide to Crystals.* Walking Stick Press, 2003.

Hamilton, Edith. *Mythology.* New York: Warner Books, 1999.

Haskins, James. *Voodoo & Hoodoo.* New York: Original Publications, 1978.

Hauck, Dennis William. *Haunted Places: The National Directory.* New York: Penguin Books, 1996.

Hendricks, Rhoda A. *Classical Gods and Heroes: Myths as Told by the Ancient Authors*. New York: Morrow Quill Paperbacks, 1974.

Holland, Eileen. *The Wicca Handbook*. York Beach, ME: Samuel Weiser, 2000.

Holland, Eileen, and Cerelia. *A Witch's Book of Answers*. York Beach, ME: Weiser Books, 2003.

Jordan, Michael. *Encyclopedia of Gods; Over 2,500 Deities of the World*. New York: Facts on File, 1993.

Knight, Sirona. *Dream Magic*. San Francisco: HarperSanFrancisco, 2000.

Malbrough, Ray T. *Charms, Spells & Formulas*. St. Paul, MN: Llewellyn Publications, 2001.

Martinez, David, Ph.D. *The Legends & Lands of Native North Americans*. New York: Sterling Publishing, 2003.

McCoy, Edain. *Celtic Myth & Magick*. St. Paul, MN: Llewellyn Publications, 2002.

Monaghan, Patricia. *The Encyclopedia of Celtic Mythology and Folklore*. New York: Facts On File, 2004.

———. *The New Book of Goddesses & Heroines*. St. Paul, MN: Llewellyn Publications, 2000.

Moura, Ann. *Green Witchcraft: Folk Magic, Fairy Lore & Herb Craft*. St. Paul, MN: Llewellyn Publications, 2001.

Ono, Sokyo. *Shinto: The Kami Way*. Tuttle Publishing, 2003.

Pickering, David. *Cassell Dictionary of Superstitions*. London: Cassell, 1995.

Roberts, Jeremy. *Japanese Mythology A to Z*. New York: Facts on File, 2004.

Steiger, Brad. *Real Ghosts, Restless Spirits, and Haunted Places*. Detroit, MI: Visible Ink Press, 2003.

Wilkinson, Philip. *Illustrated Dictionary of Mythology: Heroes, Heroines, Gods and Goddesses from Around the World*. New York: DK Publishing, 1998.

Wilkinson, Richard H. *The Complete Gods and Goddesses of Ancient Egypt*. New York: Thames & Hudson, 2003.

Zimmerman, John Edward. *Dictionary of Classical Mythology*. Bantam Books, 1971.

Zimmerman, Larry J. *American Indians: The First Nations*. London: Duncan Baird Publishers, 2003.